A

Caregiver's

Companion

Cover and text design by Brian C. Conley

ISBN 0-87793-673-0

Contents

Acknowledgments

First of all, I would like to thank God for the health and strength to complete this book.

I dedicate this book to my mom and dad. This book is for you.

No book writes itself. I am especially grateful to Mrs. Martha D. Becker. Her fifteen years of experience as a director of religious education and her long experience in training persons for various ministries are contained in this book. Without her interest, organizational talents, and confidence in this book, I doubt if it would have been completed. Her emotional support and practical suggestions were most helpful.

I have also been blessed with the encouragement and assistance of a "team" of seventeen readers who contributed to the revision of this book. I am indebted to this team who patiently read every word, offering perspective criticisms, gently pointing out unclear passages, and helping me to make corrections.

I am grateful to Bishop Donald W. Trautman, S.T.D., S.S.L., for the patient encouragement and support he has given me as this book became a reality.

Above all, I give thanks for the inspiration and guidance of the Holy Spirit throughout this writing process.

Foreword

*"What began as visits to other patients who shared the
same floor with me at Loyola Medical Center has
since blossomed into a wonderful
and life-giving ministry."*

—Joseph Cardinal Bernardin

As Cardinal Bernardin's final ministry was born of his experience in associating with the seriously ill, so *A Caregiver's Companion* draws from the personal and pastoral experience of its author, Fr. J. Daniel Dymski.

A Caregiver's Companion is really more than an operational manual. It is informative reading for all those approaching the senior years of their lives to alert them to an understanding of the changes that may be about to take place. In that same sense *A Caregiver's Companion* merits reading by entire families as well. Such a reading is not in any way meant to prepare for the worst; rather it will help all readers to recognize the latent gifts in older adults and in themselves.

Of course *A Caregiver's Companion* will be of great service to those who are already engaged in ministries with older adults. Uncounted and usually unheralded thousands of parishioners are already engaged in these ministries, for example as extraordinary ministers of the eucharist, home delivery of meals, assistance at the time of bereavement, and in many other ways. *A Caregiver's Companion* also merits careful reading on the part of pastors, pastoral staffs, and parish councils designed to initiate and direct ministries to older adults.

As with Cardinal Bernardin, we are grateful to Fr. Dymski for translating his own experiences in order to bring our present and sometimes scattered efforts on behalf of older adults into a more single focus. Our best wishes for him and for those who are moved into older adult ministry by this book.

—**Most Reverend Michael J. Murphy**
Retired Bishop of the Diocese of Erie, Pennsylvania

Introduction

The Purpose of This Book

The main purpose of this book is to provide guidance and training to pastoral caregivers serving parishioners who are homebound or in care facilities. This ministry is primarily directed to older adults and is often served by lay people with little formal training. This book is meant to fill that void.

Pastoral caregivers are called to be agents of mercy and compassion as they accompany their fellow parishioners during difficult days. This ministry focuses primarily on the spiritual needs of older adults; it is not directed to their physical and social needs.

The sections of this book help the pastoral caregiver to first understand the need for this ministry, to discern their own skills in this area, and to consider several ways to approach the situations that may arise as they undertake this ministry.

This book is practical and pedestrian in approach. It is meant to provide vital information and helpful aids to those who have taken up this ministry. It is also intended to enable these ministers to unwrap the spiritual gifts they received in baptism and confirmation in order to bring encouragement, spiritual comfort, and support to others in special need.

A Note to Parish Staff

This book is mostly intended for volunteers who visit older adult parishioners as eucharistic ministers and in the spirit of genuine friendship. However, it is helpful if a member of the pastoral staff is assigned to coordinate this ministry, perhaps under the title "Older Adult Ministry Coordinator." If this person is not professionally trained, he or she will usually work under the supervision of the pastor or associate pastor. He or she should have some basic qualities and be able to perform several basic tasks.

Qualities. Foremost, this person should be interested and sensitive to the needs of older adults and able to accept and affirm them. The coordinator should have a flexible style of leadership with the ability to adapt to many different circumstances. He or she should also possess other basic organizational skills, including the ability to lead others.

Tasks. The following tasks can form the basis of a "job description" for an Older Adult Ministry Coordinator:

- recruit pastoral caregivers
- provide opportunities for training for pastoral caregivers (and to be personally updated in the intricacies of this ministry)
- plan a program and strategies to meet the needs of older adults in the parish
- match pastoral caregivers with care receivers (older adults)
- serve as a liaison between the pastor, pastoral caregivers, and older adults
- evaluate programming and make adjustments as needed

Above all, the coordinator should have a working knowledge of the material in this book and be able to communicate its essential message to the pastoral caregivers.

Pastoral Care for Older Adults

1

A Basic Need

As we enter the third millennium, more adults sixty-five years and older are living apart from their extended families than at any time in history. And this number is only going to increase (see page 17). The situation creates a challenge both for society and the church.

A response of the United States government was the approval of an older Americans act designed to provide various forms of assistance and support to the aging population. For example, an increasing number of government-assisted nursing homes, senior living facilities, and long-term care facilities provide services including not only food and shelter, but also social, psychological, emotional, and physical services as well. Pending legislation also mandates that these facilities respond to the pastoral needs of their residents. This is where churches come in as they attempt to respond to the spiritual needs not only of those older adults in care facilities, but those who are confined to their own homes.

Many parishes currently have set up pastoral programs to meet the daily needs of some of their older members. Some parishes have a regular group of eucharistic ministers who take communion to the homebound and to those in nursing homes and hospitals. More and more parishes are recognizing the need for a more comprehensive pastoral ministry that includes spiritual formation and ways for the older adult to remain in contact with the rest of the parish community.

The ministry of *lay* pastoral caregivers is emerging as the older adult population increases and the number of clergy decreases. Lay pastoral caregivers are in need of training and formation as they undertake this worthwhile and crucial ministry.

Elderly Population

- Americans 85 and older are the nation's fastest growing age group.

- From 1960 to 1990 this group increased by more than 200 percent, compared with a gain of less than 100 percent for those 65 and older.

- By 2050, the 85-and-over population is expected to be six times the 1990 size.

Source: August 1997, U. S. Census Bureau Report

The Hands of God

Many kind and compassionate people hesitate to visit older adults because they are not sure of what to say or do when they visit. Often the simple gift of your presence is the best gift you can offer an older adult on your visit.

Older adults who are in touch with the outside community feel loved and wanted. The stimulus of a pastoral visit improves the quality and often the duration of their lives.

A pastoral caregiver brings hope in the time of need to an older adult. By your presence, you share your common belief in Jesus Christ and the good news he preached. Studies have shown that maintaining one's religious belief can make a very significant difference in the lives of older adults, including in the success of their recovery. For example, a Northwestern University study tested a group of thirty women over age sixty-five who had hip surgery. The results showed a high correlation between the extent of religious belief and the speed of recovery. Those who had strong religious beliefs were less depressed and recovered more rapidly.

As a pastoral caregiver you should recognize that your actions are prayer in motion. Mother

Teresa used to tell the story of a nurse who compared her large, squat hands to the elegant hands with delicate long fingers of a woman musician.

"I wish I had beautiful hands like yours," the nurse said to the musician. "Mine are so ugly." Before the other woman could reply, Mother Teresa said, "Your hands are among the most beautiful in the world because God is using them to do *his* work."

When you are ministering to the sick, the homebound, or anyone else in need, your hands become the hands of God—gentle, compassionate, and caring.

Part of a pastoral caregiver's ministry is to be a hand holder, both figuratively and literally. You know how a child clings to a parent's hand in a difficult situation. The hand of the pastoral caregiver is equally comforting to an older adult.

Pastoral caregivers, as representatives of the church, must be familiar with and able to respond to the needs of older adults. Often caregivers need to mediate between impersonal government or private service providers and real live people. This also means that caregivers must familiarize themselves with the intricacies of health and social service providers to determine how they can best help the older adults they visit.

Ministry to older adults should be expansive, not limiting. Some older adults live in unsafe neighborhoods and substandard housing. It is important to remember that Jesus came to serve the needs of all and that pastoral caregiving to older adults should include all of the older adults on the parish rolls.

Beatitudes for Older Adults

Blessed are they who understand
when I keep telling the same stories
over and over.

Blessed are they who know
that my ears today can't hear as once they did.

Blessed are they who seem to know
that my eyes are bright, but my mind is slow.

Blessed are they who looked away
and didn't notice my wrinkles today.

Blessed are they with a cheery smile
who encouraged me to try once more.

Blessed are they who never say,
"You asked me that question twice today."

Blessed are they who know the ways
and ignore the frustration which
releases my tension.

Blessed are they who make me know
that I'm loved, respected, and not alone.

Blessed are they who know
that I'm at a loss to put my thoughts
into words,
I get mixed up at times.

Blessed are they who ease the days
too often filled with pain and loneliness.

Blessed are they who listen,
for I still have something to say.

Blessed are they who love
me, just me, for what I am.
Your love sustains me.

I am getting older, dear loving God,
but that's all right, isn't it?

Thank you for the years so quickly gone by.

Make me ready to see you and
all my loved ones.

*Getting older means that soon I
can be with you.*

*In heaven no one gets older,
but stays forever young, and always
loved by you,
my great and dearly loved God.*

Amen.

Profile of an Older Adult

The following is an excerpt from an article by Mary Steitz that appeared in the August 1995 issue of The Eucharistic Minister. *The profile of "Emma" and other residents offers an insight into some of the issues and difficulties faced by older adults as well as the responsibilities of pastoral caregivers.*

One of the residents I have been taking communion to is Emma. I visited her for more than a year before discovering she was legally blind. Vision problems do increase with age. However, the changes happen gradually, so individuals usually are able to adapt. I asked Emma how she was always able to greet me by name when I walked in her room. She told me that my bright red coat was her first clue, then she distinguished my size and shape and my cheery voice. As the eyes age, vision may be impaired in dim light and panoramic vision may be affected. You may see older adults hold objects at a distance to focus on them. Also the lenses become harder, more opaque and yellow, allowing less light to pass through.

Notice the lighting in the room when you take communion. Because of general poorer vision and lens change, an older adult needs three times the amount of light that a younger person needs to see the same material. To assist those with failing eyesight, wear bright-colored clothing so they can "see" you better. (As people age, the colors blue, green, and gray look similar to their aging eye.) Always greet them in the exact same way so they "recognize" your welcome, as well as your voice. If you are bringing a bulletin or reading material try to have it in large print (easily done by enlarging on a copy machine) or recorded on audio. Another thing I often notice is dirty eye glasses. What a simple procedure it is to take a soft cloth and wipe glasses clean allowing clearer vision. When speaking, make sure that there is light in the room and on your face. Be aware of glare and offer to close drapes if necessary.

Another resident, Mr. Joe, always has a big smile for me when I come into his room. Because he is hard of hearing I always make sure that I'm facing him at eye level before I begin to speak. Hearing loss, perhaps more than any other physical loss, will have the greatest effect on a person's ability to relate to others. This condition affects twice as many men than women and 30 percent of persons over the age of sixty-five. Even mild hearing loss can leave a person feeling isolated and frustrated.

If you know someone is hard of hearing, instead of speaking louder, deepen your voice and speak slightly slower than you normally would. If the response is inappropriate (subtle clue that they did not hear you correctly), paraphrase using different words to say the same thing.

Other ways to enhance your visit include: face the person, get their attention by touch or eye contact, never approach from behind, use short phrases and your body language, and eliminate as much background noise as possible. It is sometimes necessary to ask if the person minds you turning down or off a radio or television set. Often a person needs to be motivated to try a hearing aid and a telephone amplifier. Beware that the hearing impaired older adult is often ignored or considered to have Alzheimer's disease or a related dementia. It is so well worth the time it takes to get to know those with hearing impairments. Their stories are also treasures.

Elsie has taught me the importance of touch. She always welcomes me with outstretched hands ready for a hug. Most older adults in long-term care settings have lost their touch partner. Their spouse, friends, and siblings have often died before them, but their need for physical contact has not diminished. Greet those you visit with an embrace, either a hug or handshake depending on their comfort level. Often they will not initiate physical contact, so I try to read their body language. Because of generalized thinning and the dryness of aging skin, itching and bruising may be present. Lotions or emollients help lubricate and hydrate the skin. While you are sharing prayers you can gently rub their hands with lotion.

Helen was a new resident I was visiting for the first time. After I reverently offered her the host, she took it back out of her mouth and broke it into small pieces. She told me that her mouth was always dry and it was so hard to swallow. Maintaining adequate fluid intake is essential and often overlooked in the older adult. After that incident I always offer everyone a glass of water or some liquid when I begin and finish our visit. It's not been uncommon to have someone drink an entire glass of water followed by a look of gratitude.

As I continue to reach people through their aging senses, I try to bring a pleasant smell into their rooms. Scents and sights of the seasons can be brought in spring, summer, fall, and winter—soft pussy willow buds, a bouquet of forsythia, garden roses, fall leaves, and evergreens have all been appreciated. One of my favorite comments came from Marie who said, "I really can't smell anymore, but I can remember how sweet and wonderful they used to smell. Thank you for that memory." Another technique that can be used is to bring the outside in by describing the weather, color changes, cold blustery wind, sparkling snowflakes, or warm sunshine.

What a privilege it is to share our Lord to those who are close to him. I have learned the most from listening to those I serve. Take the time to patiently listen. It is so worth the effort to find out what sensor losses are being experienced and think of new ways to communicate.

Spiritual Development of Older Adults

Pastoral caregivers to older adults should be familiar with the nature of late-life spirituality. Issues like loss and death color much of the spiritual development of older adults. The issue of life after death must also be fully explored.

Also, the deaths of friends and contemporaries are frequent reminders of one's own mortality. The nearness of approaching death may cause older adults to try to bring closure to several areas of their own lives.

An older adult's spirituality should include serious preparation for death as death is the time we return to God. Such an important moment deserves one's full attention and concern. As a younger person prepares for the choice for a vocation and career, so too an older person must prepare for death and eternal life. It is wrong for anyone to be so preoccupied with the work of this world as to ignore life with God in eternity.

One way to prepare for death is to put things aside and step back from earthly involvements. The process of aging usually diminishes a person's desire to be busy, or to be doing "something" all of the time. As we grow older we are not as interested in trying to impress others in the "keeping up with the Jones'" mentality. Rather, faith and spiritual development take on new significance, focusing on what is essential. What is essential is prayer and reflection on the nearness of being with God face to face for all of eternity.

Most people consciously or unconsciously abhor old age. For a deeper spiritual life, older adults must confront their feelings about their bodies' physical decline.

The spirituality of older adults is impacted heavily by physical concerns. Older adults do not have as much energy as they once did. Vision and hearing begin to deteriorate. Arthritis may affect everyday activities like threading a needle, brushing teeth, opening a jar, or kneeling for prayer. Memory loss may occur more or less regularly, affecting even prayer. Older adults may even feel what is known as a "dark night of the soul." The patience that was once a part of their personality may be gone. Spiritual devotions and prayers that were once so vital and moving, no longer have the same effect. Older adults may join with the psalmist who asks God to bring back the "joy of my youth."

How can older adults respond to these losses

associated with growing older? Can they accept these losses? Can they believe that God truly loves them even when God takes away their physical and spiritual gifts? Can these gifts be offered up in a spirit of joy? Older people are invited to a new type of prayer—a prayer of offering that goes like this:

God takes my health and my prayer says yes.

God takes my energies and my prayer says yes.

God takes my meaningful work and my prayer says yes.

The Lord gives, and the Lord takes away;

blessed be the Name of the Lord.

More Challenges

Older adults tend to become more absorbed in the past. Positive memories can help one relish the events of his or her life. The danger of becoming absorbed in these memories is that the person misses the opportunities of the present: to open their lives up to something new and rich—new people, interesting new areas of knowledge, new pains to

understand and deal with, and new ways to understand how God is present to them.

Another challenge for older adults is to find
new value in life. Some people only find value in
the work they do or how productive they are. As a
result they feel that they are less valuable when
their working days are over. In these situations pastoral caregivers can remind older adults of Jesus'
friends, Martha and Mary (see Luke 10:38-42).
Recall that Martha was the woman who was "bur-
dened with much serving" when Jesus came to
visit. Mary, on the other hand, sat beside Jesus and
listened to him speak. Jesus told the anxious
Martha that in her prayerful listening to Jesus,
Mary had chosen the "better part." Pastoral caregivers can help older adults appreciate that there is
something precious and holy in waking up each
morning to a new day and that even the simple
actions of eating, breathing, and walking are to be
treasured. As with the prayer of Mary, the prayer of
older adults is a great treasure. How good it is that
older adults have the opportunity to pray and give
glory to God.

Our society rewards independence. For those who
are aging, a challenge is to learn to be dependent.
Older adults who are open to receiving allow oth-

ers the opportunity to be kind, patient, generous, and holy themselves. When older people "decrease" it provides the opportunity for those who help them to "increase" (see John 1:29-34). Older adults need to believe that God is drawing good from their "weakness."

Aging allows the opportunity to not only receive from others, but also from God. Older adults may have spent their entire lives with the emphasis on giving to God in prayer, service, and almsgiving. But due to a change in their health conditions, they may not have the energy to offer God much in prayer or work. They need to see that by letting go and letting God guide them they are able to be more open to accepting God's will for their lives.

God builds his kingdom in ways that are not of this world, through weakness not strength. As death draws nearer, older adults must rely even more on the gift of faith.

The Golden Years
(author unknown)

*Let us take note that it is the old apple trees that are
decked with the loveliest blossoms;*

That it is the ancient redwoods that rise to majestic heights;

*That it is the old violins that produce the
richest tones;*

That it is the old wine that tastes the sweetest;

That it is for ancient coins, old stamps, antique furniture that many eagerly seek;

*That it is when the day is far spent that displays the
beauteous colors of the sunset;*

That it is when the year is old and has run its course that Mother Nature transforms the world into a fairyland of snow;

That old friends are the dearest and that it is the old people who have been loved by God for a long, long time.

Thank God for the blessing of old age—its faith, its hope, its patience, its wisdom, its experience, its maturity.

When all is said and done, OLD is wonderful!

2

Profile of Pastoral Caregivers

Fostering Holiness

The more public a ministry, the greater its responsibility to foster holiness in others. A person who volunteers as a pastoral caregiver must be someone who is forgiving, compassionate, generous, and willing to sacrifice his or her individual interests to serve the needs of older adults.

A fundamental prerequisite for pastoral caregivers is self-acceptance. Only a person who is comfortable with himself or herself is able to work maturely in shared ministry. Pastoral caregivers must be humble about their tasks and willing to elicit constructive feedback from others supporting and working alongside them in the ministry. There are several basic qualities of a pastoral caregiver, each rooted in Jesus' mission to serve and not be served (see Mark 10:42). They are:

- *selflessness*, with the ability to focus on the welfare of another;
- *sensitivity*, the quality of recognizing and responding to the needs and emotional state of others;
- *approachability*, including being available even when inconvenient, and possessing a friendly, warm, and nonjudgmental attitude;
- *flexibility*, especially in being tolerant of the points of view of others and having a willingness to look at things in new ways;
- *responsibility* in being able to carry through on commitments;
- *self-discipline* to stay with a difficult task;
- *creativity* to envision, plan, and take the ministry in new and positive directions;
- *communication skills* to be able to speak clearly and to listen well;
- *sense of humor* to laugh at one's own mistakes and to break the tension in a relationship with an appropriate story, phrase, word, or action;

- *a deep spirituality* to communicate to others through words, actions, and demeanor;
- *confidentiality*, respecting what is told in private conversations;
- *affirming*, with the ability to see and express the good in others.

Self-Evaluation for Pastoral Caregivers

The following questions can help you evaluate yourself for the ministry of a pastoral caregiver.

- *What are my gifts?*
- *What are my weaknesses and limitations?*
- *How can I grow spiritually to help my ability to minister?*
- *What are my reasons for wanting to work in this ministry?*
- *How is this ministry self-serving?*
- *How is this ministry self-giving?*
- *How does this ministry help me to know more deeply God and church?*
- *Which words best describe how I feel when I visit an older person (name other words): lonely,*

*loss of control, despair, physical pain, insecurity,
denial, anger, rejection, frustration, embarrassment, boredom, restlessness, confusion, aban-
donment, fatigue, fright, hopelessness, happy,
helpful, fulfilled?*
• *Is it truly God's will that I serve in this ministry?*

*Analyze your responses. What do they tell you
about your ability to serve in this ministry? How
do you see yourself being a positive influence on
those you are called to serve?*

Pastoral Caregiver Job Description

Volunteers who seek to become pastoral caregivers for selfish reasons may not be fit for this ministry. For example, a pastoral caregiver may view
the ministry as his or her primary means for fulfill-
ment. As a result, when an older adult shares a sug-
gestion or criticism with the person he or she may
feel offended.

Some people choose involvement in various
church ministries to enhance their prestige and

self-respect. For some pastoral caregivers, the emphasis is on "me" rather than the person being ministered to. Authentic pastoral care for older people involves ministers who are other-centered, the opposite of narcissistic. The following are several tasks that may be found on a job description for a pastoral caregiver:

Tasks
- Train appropriately for the ministry;
- Care for own spiritual welfare and development;
- Visit older adults as a friend and as a eucharistic minister;
- Learn where to secure information and resources for particular requests;
- Make older adults more aware of the presence of Christ in their lives;
- Pray with the older adult and encourage him or her to pray for the minister and the ministry;
- Invoke the Holy Spirit in prayer to prepare for visits with the older adult.

Pastoral Caregiver's Bill of Rights

I have the right to . . .

- take care of myself. This is not an act of selfishness.
- seek help from others. I recognize the limits of my own endurance and strength.
- maintain my own spiritual life.
- get angry, be depressed, and express other difficult feelings occasionally.
- reject any attempt by my care receiver to manipulate me through guilt, anger, or depression.
- receive consideration, affection, forgiveness, and acceptance for what I do for my care receiver as long as I offer these qualities in return.
- take pride in what I am accomplishing and to applaud the courage it has often taken to meet the needs of my care receiver.
- honestly share how I am feeling about my ministry with other ministers without fear that confidentiality will be broken.

3 *Ministry Skills for Pastoral Caregivers*

Visits With Older Adults

In visiting older adults, you will be meeting some of the most interesting people at the most difficult time of their lives. Most of them are doing the best they can.

When you visit an older adult, always be mindful of God's presence within you. Life is prayer; all should be done for the glory and honor of God. Remain in constant conversation with God and let your visit be your way of serving God. Remember that God is present with you and with the person you visit. On your visit, the older adult should feel God's presence in a tangible way.

Here are some other suggestions for a home visit:

- Phone ahead to determine a good time for your visit. It is not wise to drop by unannounced.
- Knock on the door. When invited in, introduce yourself clearly. Give your name, where you are from, and why you are there. If your parish provides cards for identification, give this to the person who answers the door.
- Do your best to understand the correct pronunciation of the person's name. It is okay to ask the person if you are pronouncing it properly. If the correction is offered, practice until you can say the name correctly.
- Some people like to be touched and others do not. Respect the wishes of the older adult. Do not force a hug. Ask if they would like one.
- Exchange schedules and appropriate phone numbers and clarify mutual expectations about your visits. Never offer more than you can deliver.
- Let the person you are visiting choose what you do together. The person may want to play cards.
- When visiting a member of your parish, take a parish bulletin along to share with the person. If the person has impaired vision, offer to read

the bulletin to them. Writing letters for them as they dictate the letters to you is also a helpful exercise.

- Regardless of how much you may disagree with the family's way of dealing with the older adult, it is *never* appropriate to give unsolicited advice. Your responsibility is to work as helpfully and harmoniously as possible within the given structure and not try to change it. *Abuse of any kind is the exception* (see pages 114-115).

- If the older adult indicates unmet needs, it is best to discuss the situation with the person's primary caregiver or the parish staff member responsible for older adult ministry. In the meantime, tell the older adult you will try to be of help. Follow through and let the person know the results of your efforts.

- You may be asked to arrange a ride to Mass or other parish functions or a visit from a priest. It is best to check with the parish staff member before you transport the person in your own vehicle.

- Instead of saying "Let me know if you need anything," ask, "What can I do?" The latter is likely to get a response, the former is not.

- Do not be concerned about silence. Some people do not like to talk, but nevertheless appreciate having a visitor there with them. When there is silence, ask the person if they would like some background music played and if so what type.
- Older adults often repeat themselves. Do your best to listen patiently.
- You cannot take away the person's pain or stop the confusing flood of emotions. Be yourself. Sometimes the best gift you can give is to allow the older adult to just *feel* without being judged for his or her feelings.
- Do not discourage conversations about death and dying. Allow the person to express his or her feelings about this most difficult topic. Part 5, "Death, Dying, and Bereavement," offers several helps.
- Help the older adult to trust God to guide them through their struggles. Be accepting even if the person is angry with God. Remind the person that God's love for him or her is great.
- Your role is to be a friendly visitor, not an expert authority. Medical and technical ques-

tions are best referred to a nurse, physician, or pharmacist.

- A person you visit may offer you money. Politely explain that you are a pastoral volunteer and that if they wish to give money, they can donate it to the parish or a favorite charity.
- Keep your visit to an agreed upon time. You don't want to overly tire an older person or have them feel like you will never leave.

There are a few other suggestions that apply specifically to nursing home visits.

They are:

- Greet the receptionist when you arrive. Introduce yourself and tell the name of the parish you represent. Show your identification. (It is important to get to know the nursing home staff. In time they will get to know you and can provide some insights to help you in your ministry.)
- When walking the halls take time to greet all the residents, even if they are not the person you came to visit. All people are God's children and worthy of your time and attention. In addition,

they are co-residents, perhaps even friends, of the person you are visiting. A kind word from you might be the highlight of their day.

- When entering a room, knock on the door and wait until you are invited in.
- If you wish to take a food treat to the older adult, be sure to check with the staff about any food restrictions and limitations.

These suggestions may be used in any order and in a variety of different situations. Don't forget to assert your rights. You have a right not to be the recipient of excessive demands from the care receiver, anger which is inappropriately directed at you, or requests for advice which cannot be deflected using the suggestions above or with the skills that follow.

Communication Skills

Although we communicate constantly there are specific skills that can help anyone to improve *how* they communicate.

As a pastoral caregiver it is important for you to keep the focus of communication on the person you are visiting. It is all right to talk about yourself—

since sharing some of your experiences helps build rapport between you and the one you are visiting—but you need to be conscious of not monopolizing the discussion.

A first step in good communication is to put aside your own problems and concerns so that you can focus clearly on the person you are visiting. It is also important to be aware of your own feelings and prejudices so that they do not interfere with your visit. Perhaps you are uncomfortable talking about death or have had a difficult experience while visiting a nursing home in the past. You may have strong feelings about lifestyles or values different from your own. Being aware of these feelings can help you establish an honest rapport with the person you are visiting. Some related communication skills follow.

Body Language

The messages given by our body language communicates a great deal about us. There are several ways your body language can enhance your visit with an older adult. For example:

- Try to main eye-level contact with the older person, however do not stare. Stand when the person is standing, sit when he or she is sitting. (Standing over a person often can be read as asserting power.)

- When sitting, do so in a relaxed manner, perhaps leaning forward slightly to show your interest. (Do not fidget. This indicates you are eager to end the visit.)
- Keep your hands relaxed, perhaps in your lap. Avoid crossing your arms on your chest. This may give the impression you are being defensive to what is being said. Do not point a finger at the older adult. This may imply accusation.
- Be aware of the distance between yourself and the other person. Everyone has a "safe zone" which is threatened if someone invades it. When the older person pulls back or moves suddenly away from you, this may be an indication that you have entered his or her space.

Beginning a Conversation

Beginning a conversation with someone you have only recently met can be difficult. The following suggestions can help you get started:

- Greet the older adult with a formal title (Mr. or Mrs.). Using a first name greeting may be interpreted as patronizing. It is only appropriate when you know the person well.

- Identify yourself and the reason for your visit: "I'm from St. Mary's Parish. I came to see you because I volunteered to be a pastoral caregiver." Or, "I am here to bring you holy communion." Or, "I came because we miss you." Show your parish identification as appropriate.

- Use phrases like, "I am looking forward to getting to know you better," or "I've been looking forward to seeing you again," or "Tell me something about yourself." Let the person know you are available to them.

- Begin conversations with broad openings and general compliments like "How are you doing?" or "You're looking better today." Avoid asking questions that can be answered with one word.

- If the person you are visiting has a hearing impairment, speak in a lower tone and slowly and make the point of facing the person. Don't raise your voice at all older adults assuming everyone who is older has trouble hearing. This isn't true.

Active Listening

Active listening describes a technique of letting the person you are having a conversation with really know that you are listening. Some of the skills of active listening are:

- Phrases like "Yes, go on," "That's interesting," or "Oh, really, tell me more" let the person know you are following the conversation.

- Asking open-ended questions tells the person you wish them to continue. For example, "What happened next?" or "How did you manage?" Open-ended questions often begin with the pronouns who, what, where, when, why, or how. However, avoid asking too many questions. The person may feel like you're running an inquisition and quit talking.

- Restating what the person has told you provides clarity and focus in the conversation and establishes that you are following the story. Restatement sentences often begin with phrases like, "Let me be sure I understand what you said . . . " or "What I hear you saying is . . . " followed by your summary statement. If you are not on target the person will clarify what was meant. If you are, the person will continue.

- When the speaker's perception of reality seems unlikely, it may be appropriate to voice this doubt by saying something like, "That seems really unusual," or "Really? That seems difficult to believe." The goal is to encourage the speaker to evaluate the perception, not to impose your judgment of reality.

Empathetic Listening

Empathetic listening involves putting yourself into the speaker's position to really understand what he or she is feeling. Each person experiences a situation in a unique way. No one feels exactly the same about any given situation. The goal of empathetic listening is to identify with the speaker and what the speaker is saying. Some techniques of empathetic listening are:

- Always try to keep your response simple and concrete.
- The voice of the person you are talking with can give you a clue to their feelings. For example, increased volume could signify excitement or

anger, lower volume could signify discomfort, embarrassment, or shame.

- Do not judge a person's tears. Often the tears are uncontrollable and do not signify what you imagine.
- Let the person express himself or herself. It may be helpful to ask the speaker to describe his or her feelings. For example, "Why do you feel anxious?" or "Why are you frightened?" are good beginnings.
- Help the person compare the current experience with some previous experiences he or she may have had. Ask things like "Have you had a similar experience?" or "Have you felt like this before?" These questions will help the person place the current experience into the big life picture.
- Responding to questions that ask you for advice can be difficult, especially for those whose personality leads them to want further involvement. It is helpful to remember that your goals are to acknowledge the speaker's point of view *and* his or her ability to make a decision. Giving advice undermines the speaker

and puts the listener in control. Rather, asking a second question which repeats the speaker's original question is preferable. For example:

"Do you think I should tell the doctor?"

Response: "Do you think you should?"

"What should I tell my daughter about the problem?"

Response: "What do you think you should tell her?"

Remember, the goals of empathetic listening are to establish rapport with the older adult and to bring Christ to him or her. It is not appropriate to delve more deeply into the person's life or to try to counsel. Counseling is for professionals. Empathetic listening can help the older adult clarify feelings, grow in acceptance, and draw on the total life experience to deal appropriately with given situations.

Assertive Language

Being assertive helps you to set limits and let the older adult know of your personal feelings, wants, needs, and limits in a manner which respects the other person and does not hurt his or her dignity.

Assertive language means using "I" messages to let the other person know your position without judging his or her position. "I" messages coupled with an explanation help the other person understand how his or her behavior affects you. For example, "When you ask me to stay longer I feel sad because, though I would like to stay and visit, my ride is here. So let's say good-bye with a smile and look forward to our next meeting."

Other "I" messages begin with phrases like these:

- I like . . .
- I feel . . .
- I want . . .
- I am interested to know . . .
- I do (not) like it when . . .
- I am able to . . .

Effective Problem Solving

You will inevitably be asked to solve a problem so always keep the limits of your role in mind. Some basic steps for problem solving are:

- Learning about the problem.
- Defining the problem.
- Generating and evaluating options for response.
- Choosing a course of action.
- Taking action.
- Evaluating the outcome.

Help the older adult through this process, analyzing the options at each step. Ask questions like "Have you thought of . . . ?" or "What do you think would happen if . . . ?" and encourage the person to make his or her own choice.

Statement of Confidentiality

Pastoral caregivers frequently learn a great deal about the older adults they visit including many details about their personal lives, spiritual well-being, and medical problems. Out of respect, *no* information about the older adult may be shared with any other person or agency. The exceptions are:

- A third party—a parish staff person or spouse of the caregiver—should know the name,

address, phone number, and time when you are
visiting the older adult so the person can be
contacted in case of an emergency.

- When the older adult has a spiritual request—
such as the desire to receive the sacraments—
these should be communicated to a priest or
someone on the parish staff.

- Signs of depression or suicidal statements
should be brought to the attention of the primary caregiver. If the person is in a nursing
home or hospital, talk to the nursing staff. If
the person is homebound, talk to a family
member. If a family member is not available
talk to a priest or parish staff member.

- If the person shows signs of being abused physically, sexually, or through neglect, report this to a
priest or parish staff member.

Unfortunately the suicide rate is increasing
more rapidly in older adults than in any other seg-
ment of the population. No one needs to suffer
needlessly without receiving help. You may be the
one who can help. Further information on elder
abuse is available on pages 114-115 and through
your local agency on aging.

The Right of Privacy
Written by Chaplain Bernadette Sullivan, O.S.B., B.C.C.,
and members of the Department of Pastoral Services of
Hamot Medical Center,
Erie, Pennsylvania

As a pastoral caregiver it must be your top priority to be mindful that the **right of privacy is a sacred right that each individual is entitled to.** *When you are visiting older adults or their families remember that what they tell you, even in the most basic conversations, should not be repeated to anyone else unless you have received permission to do so. Even to mention to someone that "Mary is in the hospital" is a breach of confidentiality. If you want to tell someone that Mary is in the hospital, first ask Mary. Say, "Mary, would you mind if I told Mrs. Jones that you are in the hospital?" Mary may or may not care. But she must be given the choice to what information is shared with others.*

There will be times when other parishioners may ask you about the condition or some other information about someone you have visited. Any answer should be so ambiguous that it does not reveal any confidential information. A proper response might be, "I am in no position to answer that question, perhaps you should ask Mary yourself or one of her family members."

Remember: all information you glean from a visit with an older adult is private unless the person gives you express permission to share it with others.

Whether your visit is to a person's private home or a nursing home, treasure the opportunity to visit. It is an opportunity to grow in tolerance, patience, compassion, and understanding of the limitless power of love. Although it requires concentration and hard work, you are likely to gain as much from the relationship as the person you are visiting. Above all, enjoy your visit. You may wish to end a visit with a Bible passage like the following message from God to Moses (based on Numbers 6:24-26):

May the Lord bless you and keep you!

May the Lord let his face shine upon you, and be gracious to you!

May the Lord look upon you kindly and give you peace!

Amen.

Praying With Older Adults

Beginning to Pray

How often do you hear or say, "I'll pray for you"? Do you think the others really follow up with their promise? Do you? Praying for others is an important part of the Christian vocation. Pastoral caregivers are encouraged to pray for and with others, including the older adults they visit.

As you prepare to pray with others it will be helpful to pray and reflect on how you personally experience God's love. Through the graces received in baptism and confirmation, God works through you. You experience God's love as grace that continually moves through your life in powerful and unseen ways. If you open yourself in deep humility to God, you can open the door to grace by trusting God. As you form the habit of trusting God in

small details, it will become easier to trust God
with your deeper concerns.

Because people experience God's love through
others, it is important to encourage one another.
According to a native American saying, "One kind
word can warm a whole winter." Perhaps you can
think of a time when a kind comment, compli-
ment, an expression of love, or a word of comfort
lifted your spirits and gave you new hope. Phrases
like "You look great today," or "You'll do a terrific
job," spoken by a friend, family member, or co-
workers can make your day. Encouraging others
can keep you open to the Spirit in your own life. By
your willingness to cooperate with God and to
open your heart to God, you are letting God's
power and grace flow through your own life to the
lives of others. Pastoral caregivers need to have a
personal prayer life before they can pray for and
with others. You can only give to others what you
have received yourself from God in prayer.

Ways to Pray

Prayer can be difficult at all stages of life. With
the number of losses that older adults suffer and
with illness consuming a great amount of their

energy, it is no surprise that praying might be difficult for them. It is helpful for a pastoral caregiver to remember these hardships and not be put off by an older adult who finds it nearly impossible to pray.

There are many ways of praying with others. Some pastoral caregivers feel most comfortable reading aloud from the scriptures (ask the person if he or she has a favorite they would like you to read) or a prayer book. Others prefer praying traditional prayers like the Our Father, Hail Mary, or Memorare. If the older adult has little energy to pray, you can ask the person to listen to short prayers, aspirations, or a litany (see the Resource Section, pages 121-166). Encourage spontaneous prayers, especially prayers of thanks for the good the person has already received in life. Silent time is also a form of prayer. Pray in silence that the Lord will accomplish his will in you and the older adult. Consider also the meditative practice of a centering prayer or a quiet repetition of a short prayer phrase to help you and the person you are visiting focus more clearly on God's will and God's love. Centering prayer is so named because it allows us to enter into the deepest center of ourselves.

Seventeenth-Century Nun's Prayer
(The title of this prayer is traditional; the source is unknown.)

Lord, Thou knowest better than I know myself that I am growing older and will someday be old. Keep me from the fatal habit of thinking I must say something on every subject and on every occasion. Release me from the craving to straighten out everybody's affairs. Make me thoughtful but not moody; helpful but not bossy. With my vast store of wisdom, it seems a pity not to use it all, but Thou knowest Lord, that I want a few friends at the end.

Keep my mind free from the recital of endless details; give me wings to get to the point. Seal my lips on my aches and pains. They are increasing and love of rehearsing them is becoming sweeter as the years go by. I dare not ask for grace enough to enjoy the tales of others' pains, but help me to endure them with patience.

I dare not ask for improved memory, but for growing humility and a lessening cocksureness when my memory seems to clash with the memories of others. Teach me the glorious lesson that occasionally I may be mistaken.

Keep me reasonably sweet; I do not want to be a saint—some of them are hard to live with—but a sour old person is one of the crowning works of the devil. Give me the ability to see good things in unexpected places, and talents in unexpected people. And, give me O Lord, the grace to tell them so.

Amen.

Prayer in the Time of Illness

When a person is ill, the pastoral caregiver's presence is more important than ever. Pray for the ill person quietly and contemplatively. Gently touch the person on the forehead, perhaps lightly tracing the Sign of the Cross. Jesus physically touched those who were sick. You may want to rub the arm or hold the hand of the sick person. Remind the person of Jesus' love for him or her. Don't extend your visit when someone is sick. Sick people tire easily and need to conserve energy.

Prayer is a way through troubled times. Prayer is not a magic wand to cure all infirmities, pain, and illness, but prayer can make these hardships more bearable. Prayer may or may not alter the person's physical illness, but it will certainly dramatically change the way a person copes with an illness. It is important to understand and to be able to communicate the distinction between praying for healing and praying for an acceptance of God's will. Some people who are ill *only* pray for healing and feel not praying for a cure is tantamount to giving up. The prayer of Jesus in the garden—"My Father, if it is not possible that this cup pass without my drinking it, your will be done!" (Matthew 26:42)—is a good reminder of the distinction between these types of prayer.

Further, you may have an older adult ask you, "Why am I made to suffer? I have been praying for healing, but God has not answered my prayers." God always answers prayer, but God doesn't always answer "yes." The reasons for suffering and pain are a great mystery. Jesus never explained why people must suffer. However we know from church tradition that when we suffer, we can experience the presence of Jesus' redemptive love and we can participate in Jesus' saving works. Suffering in union with Christ is a powerful form of intercessory prayer and a source of blessing for the entire church.

When praying with and for older adults you share God's healing power and love. You become a channel of divine compassion, helping the other person to be open to whatever Jesus may want them to do. Prayer reminds us that God is present.

Pray for today and leave the future to God!

The Sacrament of the Anointing of the Sick

Prior to the Second Vatican Council it was typical for a priest to be called out in the middle of the night to anoint a person who was unconscious and very near to death. In visiting with the family, the priest would discreetly ask why they didn't call him out sooner so that the person could have been coherent during the anointing. The answer typically came back, "We did not want to scare him (or her)." Or, sometimes hospital patients would ask a priest for the anointing, but also tell him not to tell the person's family for fear of upsetting them. Then while the priest went to get the oils, the family would also request some form of a "secret" anointing for the sick person!

With Vatican II, the sacrament is now called the anointing of the sick, not *extreme unction* ("final anointing"). The new rite of the sacrament encourages that it be administered near the beginning of a serious illness and repeated as complications or new illnesses develop. In the years since Vatican II there has been a growing understanding that the anointing of the sick is a sacrament of healing. The sacrament per se of the dying is *viaticum* or "food for the journey" (communion).

The sacrament of the anointing of the sick is prefigured in the New Testament (see Mark 6:12 and James 5:14-15). The text from James asks "Is anyone among you sick?" The word sick in this instance (from the Greek *asthenenei*) does not connote a grave illness. Therefore even in its earliest roots, the anointing of the sick is not only for the dying. It is important for pastoral caregivers to understand this sacrament and to be able to communicate a correct understanding to those they visit.

The sacrament of the anointing of the sick is not necessary for salvation, though no Catholic should neglect this sacrament. The proper minister of the sacrament is a priest.

Who Are the Candidates for the Sacrament?

Pastoral caregivers have an important role to play in the administration of the sacrament of the anointing of the sick in that they must recommend to the person or the person's family that he or she request the sacrament of the anointing of the sick.

It is important to remind those who wish to be anointed, including those anointed during less serious illness, that the purpose of the sacrament is to bring spiritual strength. Through this sacrament God is offering the anointed person the grace to overcome anxiety and despair, to find comfort in the suffering, and to be healed physically even if their body is diseased or broken. The sacrament of the anointing of the sick is to remind us that neither disease nor death are the end; nor are they to be feared. Sickness and death are to be faced with Christ's help.

Distributing Holy Communion Outside of Mass

An important part of the ministry for many pastoral caregivers is to bring the eucharist to older adults who are not able to come to Mass. With the eucharist pastoral caregivers bring the prayers and support of the rest of the communion of the faithful.

The eucharist should be carried to the person's home or nursing home in a pyx and placed on a table covered with a clean cloth. When appropriate the distribution of communion should be accompanied by prayer, including a penitential rite, scripture reading, and the Lord's Prayer. For reception of communion, the pastoral caregiver takes the vessel or pyx and goes directly to the communicant, raises the host slightly, and says "the Body of Christ." The person answers "Amen" and receives communion.

The Rite for Distributing Communion Outside of Mass is included on pages 121-126 of the Resource section.

Leading a Prayer Service

You may be asked to lead a prayer service in a nursing home, an extended care facility, a group home, or an apartment complex for older adults. The Resource section (pages 126-166) contains a selection from the *Pastoral Care of the Sick*

(NCCB) and several other prayer elements that may be used as part of a prayer service.

Before you lead a prayer service take note of the environment. The use of a candle, a bible, or flowers as visuals can create an appealing atmosphere for prayer. These visuals do not have to be complicated; rather, they should communicate simply the sacredness of the space where you and the group will be praying.

A prayer service should begin with a word of welcome, an opening hymn, followed by a formal opening prayer. Next, read a short passage from scripture and respond with a psalm reading or a simple hymn. You may wish to share some short personal reflections on the theme of the reading and dialogue with the participants to hear their reflections as well. General intercessions, the Lord's Prayer, and a closing hymn complete the prayer service.

5 Death, Dying, and Bereavement

Ministering to the Dying

Pastoral care to older adults inevitably involves facing the issues of death, dying, and effective ministry to the dying. In order to positively serve the dying, it is important for you to give some deep thought to the subject of death, especially as it relates to your own mortality.

You may ask yourself, "Why would I choose this ministry if it has so much to do with suffering and death?" In short, ministering to the dying is a powerful experience for a pastoral caregiver who is able to share in the final weeks, days, and minutes of a fellow, faithful Christian. You are able to enter the person's precious life space and share in a concrete way your strong conviction in the resurrection.

Today's society and culture mostly ignores, fears, or glosses over death. Everything is focused

on avoiding pain and suffering and striving only for
a better life on earth. Oppositely, Christian teaching finds meaning in suffering and death as we
share in the redemptive work of Christ. According
to the *Pastoral Care for the Sick*,

> the family and friends of the sick and those
> who take care of them, in any way, have a spe-
> cial share in this ministry of comfort. In par-
> ticular, it is their task to strengthen the sick
> with words of faith and by praying with them,
> to commend them to the suffering and glori-
> fied Lord, and to encourage them to contribute
> to the well-being of the people of God by
> associating themselves willingly with Christ's
> passion and death (paragraph 34).

The Resource section (pages 158-166) offers
suggestions for prayers of commendation, prayers
after death, and prayers for family and friends.

There is no "right" way to minister to dying
persons. The following guidelines divided into
stages of before, during, and after death are meant
as suggestions and can be adapted to match particular situations and personalities of those involved.

Before

- Before death, it is important to be present to the person on a regular basis; as much as the person wants and as frequently as your schedule permits. As you gain the person's trust, he or she will be more comfortable sharing with you his or her feelings, fears, and hopes.

- Anger is a common feeling of the dying. Be prepared to hear questions like, "Why is this happening to me?"

- As a pastoral caregiver you may be dealing with the person's family as well. Generally, family members can help make the dying process easier. However not everyone deals with dying in the same way. You may be able to help by bringing all family members together to talk and listen to one another and to share their feelings about death and dying.

- Encourage family members to allow children and grandchildren to visit the person who is dying as much as both parties are able.

- During your visits listen more than talk.

- Do not try to answer any medical questions.

- If the subject is brought up or you sense an appropriate time, offer suggestions about death planning.
- Keep the parish priest and appropriate staff person apprised of the dying person's condition.

During

- At the time of death, make sure friends and family members of the dying person are made welcome. If the person is in a shared room, ask permission of the roommate to be able to pray out loud.
- Remember to touch and talk. The senses of touch and hearing are the last to diminish as one dies. Even comatose and sedated people can feel and hear. Let the person know who is in the room. Speak directly into the person's ear. Tell the person who is touching the dying person's arm or patting a shoulder to say their name. Ask family members to do the touching: holding the person's hand, rubbing the arms, face, hair, or shoulders. Ask family members and friends to tell the dying person how much he or

she is loved. Allow some time alone between friends and family and the dying person.

- A dying person should have the opportunity to receive the sacraments of the church. Remember to maintain contact with a priest as the time of death nears.
- Remind the dying person that it is all right to "let go" because God has his arms stretched out to welcome him or her.
- Do not talk about the dying person in the past tense as though already deceased. This can be very upsetting for someone who can hear but not respond verbally.
- Do not whisper or try to talk about the dying person so that he or she cannot hear you.
- You may wish to take a sponge and moisten the person's lips, while continuing to talk. Simply saying, "I am here and I am with you" is a great sign of support and comfort.
- A dying person may be delirious a times, possibly as a result of a fever or a reaction to a medication. Or, a dying person may be confused, perhaps because of too much calcium in the blood or too little oxygen in the brain.

- A person near death may have visions of deceased relatives. He or she may even see and speak to these persons. Others may see a bright light. Dying persons often cannot put into words what they see and feel.
- Respond in encouraging terms. For example, if a dying person says, "My mother is waiting for me," merely repeat the same statement and add, "I am so glad your mother is near. Can you tell me more about it?"
- Be honest if you are having trouble understanding the dying person. You may say, "I think you are trying to tell me something important and I am trying very hard, but I am just not getting it. I will keep trying."
- Some people will delay the timing of their death, waiting to die until certain people arrive or until others leave.
- The process of dying may take place over a period of hours or even days. Even a professional medical person cannot predict when a person will die. At times, a dying person's condition may show improvement. These roller coaster changes can be difficult for those caring for the dying person.

- There are some common signs to look for as a person nears death. The person may feel clammy or damp. The color of his or her skin may take a bluish shade. The breathing pattern of the person may change. The number of times and how deeply the person breathes will lessen until the breathing stops very quietly. There may be a decrease in movement and a loss of strength. Or, the person may have a greater awareness and open their eyes or smile after not doing these things for quite a while. The dying person usually slips into death in a way similar to how he or she has fallen asleep his or her entire life. It is very unusual for a person to convulse or hemorrhage just before dying.
- Breaks with fresh air and exercise are important for the pastoral caregiver as caring for a dying person is a grueling vocation.

After

- Support the family. Help family members accept the reality of their loved one's death. Be available to listen without being obtrusive.
- Encourage the offspring of the deceased to put

aside feelings of guilt. If not addressed early on, guilt can cause a great amount of lasting emotional scars.

- Do not be reluctant to frequently mention the deceased person's name and to encourage reminiscing by family members if this is culturally appropriate.
- Keep some holy water with you. After the person has died, allow those present to sprinkle the body of the deceased with the holy water and offer a blessing.
- In a nursing home or hospital, you may call on staff who will not be able to attend the funeral to pay their last respects.
- Make an effort to attend the funeral.
- Maintain contact with the family members and friends in the days, weeks, and months afterward. Do this by phone calls, letters, and personal contact.

Meditation on Mary, the Caregiver, to Her Dying Son, Jesus

Standing by the cross of Jesus were his mother and his mother's sister, Mary the wife of Clopas, and Mary of Magdala.

—John 19:25

Mary, the mother of Jesus, like any caregiver must have felt exhausted from emotional tension. Even though Jesus' body was racked with pain, there was nothing Mary could do to help. The vocation of a caregiver calls for a life of sacrifice.

Mary gave her son life, nursed him, bathed him as an infant, did his laundry, prepared his meals, and prayed with him. Now she must let him go.

Mary stands motionless, patiently at the foot of the cross, while blood streams down and almost blinds Jesus. His eyes open and look at her. The face of Jesus is not familiar. His gray skin is shriveled and hanging loose in spots. Jesus' eyes are sunken far into his bony skull. His body once plump and rounded, is now a wasted skeleton, skin over sharp bones, barely alive. The skin has red and black spots, with circles from the marks of the leather whips. No morphine to kill the pain. Mary looks on and says to herself, "O God! How long?"

Jesus begins to lose strength. God knew what he was doing when he appointed Mary as Jesus' caregiver. God gave to Mary a heart of wax, to melt with compassion. As the caregiver, Mary waited almost three hours watching her loved one suffer.

Jesus stops breathing. There had been no painkillers to make him sleep. The heart of Mary pounds rapidly, as she waits and watches. The skies become dark. Mary prepares for death's agonizing moment. God's will be done. Mary, her sister, and Mary Magdalene cling together. They look for support from one another, to ease their stress.

Jesus gives up without a fight. Mary remembers the message about total trust in the Father's will. She recalls her son's words, "Do not let your hearts be troubled. Have faith in God and me." Mary speaks not a word of her sorrow and her fears to others, recalling an earlier time when she "treasured all these things and reflected on them in her heart" (Luke 2:19). The handmaid of the Lord had done her work.

Bereavement and Grieving

Death leaves behind a group of family members and friends who are suffering greatly over the loss of their loved one. These are the bereaved and a time of bereavement and grieving should be respected and supported by the pastoral caregiver.

There are many characteristics and reactions of a grieving person. Some of these are listed below.

- The person may experience a loss of energy or perspective.
- Sometimes a person will experience periods of disconnected crying. At those times, it is appropriate to reassure the person his or her feelings are normal.
- A person may be disoriented and lose faith in long-held beliefs.
- Depression, sorrow, and withdrawal are common.
- Some people mask their feelings and put on a brave front in public. Others will choose to remain isolated while they grieve.
- Be aware that some people use medication to block feelings.

- Some people may experience a loss of self-identity or self-worth if their identity was closely bound with the person who died. It is important to reinforce the person's individuality at a time like this.

Coping With Grief

A person who grieves is affected in many ways: psychologically, physically, socially, economically, and spiritually to name a few. Your task in working with the bereaved is to recognize unhealthy ways the person is coping in each of these areas and to gently point the bereaved to healthier ways to cope with his or her grief. Some hints for recognizing and coping with grief in various areas follow:

Psychological
- Emotions that were unexpressed in the first days after a person's death may be revealed later. It is important for a grieving person to express feelings and make his or her needs known to you. They may need to cry due to how they feel.
- Everyone needs help with grief. Be ready to offer your support. Keep in touch with the person on a regular routine.

- There is no "right" length of time to grieve. The time period varies for each person. Be available for as long as a grieving person needs you.

Physical
- A person who grieves may neglect his or her physical appearance. As you are able, you may help the person organize his or her wardrobe and toiletries.
- A grieving person also tends to neglect his or her health. This leaves the person more susceptible to disease. Remind those you minister to of the importance of eating regularly and nutritiously, of getting adequate sleep, and of exercising.
- Keeping regular medical check-ups is important for the grieving.

Social
- Friends and family members of the bereaved are often very willing to help. Look for ways to allow these people to show their support.
- Though no one can replace a person's loved one (spouse, parent, son, or daughter), social interaction with others can help to lessen the

pain. However, sometimes in an effort to stop the pain of grief, people try to "replace" the deceased person (e.g., remarriage or adoption) too soon. Remind the bereaved that it is hard to view relationships objectively when one is grieving.

- Though there is a need to allow the bereavement process to run its course before a person gets involved in a new relationship or remarries, new relationships should not be avoided because of societal or family pressures.

Economic
- Usually the person should be encouraged to remain in his or her home until the time of initial grief has passed.
- All financial decisions should be made in consultation with trusted financial advisers.
- A bereaved person should return to work. However, remind the person that work will not satisfy all his or her needs. Relationships with family and friends should not be sacrificed in an effort to keep busy.

Spiritual
- There are generally two types of faith responses to a loss of a loved one. Either a person's faith will be of great comfort, or maintaining faith may be difficult as the person questions God over the loss. Help the person work through either situation while reminding them that each type of reaction can be an opportunity for spiritual growth.

Heaven Is Our Home

Anyone is capable of going to heaven. Heaven is our home. People ask me about death and whether I look forward to it and I answer, "Of course," because I am going home. Dying is not the end, it is just the beginning. Death is a continuation of life. This is the meaning of eternal life; it is where our soul goes to God, to be in the presence of God, to see God, to speak to God, to continue loving him with all our heart and all our soul. We only surrender our body in death—our heart and soul live forever. When we die we are going to be with God, and with all those we have known and loved who have gone before us: our family and our friends will be waiting for us. Heaven must be a beautiful place.

—**Mother Teresa**
1910-1997

6 Special Circumstances in Pastoral Caregiving

Older Adults and Depression

Winston Churchill battled depression. Abraham Lincoln suffered bouts of what was then called "melancholy" that were so severe that he considered suicide. Even the scriptures tell of expressions of depression and despair. Elijah asked for his life to be taken. Jonah was deeply despondent after God did not destroy Nineveh as had been promised. Job's depression was such that his wife advised him to "curse God and die."

Older adults often experience depression to various degrees. Depression may stem from loss of health, retirement from work, the death of a spouse or close friend, or a host of other situations that go hand in hand with old age. Depression can also result from a lack of consolation in prayer.

When you interact on a regular basis with an older adult, you may notice signs of depression: loss of appetite, little energy or motivation, excessive worries and anxieties, or hopelessness. A person may even share with you his or her wish to die.

Most everyone experiences mild depression from time to time. (If you feel someone is severely depressed, seek the help of a professional.) Some types of medication can cause temporary depression. In just about every situation a person suffering from depression looks negatively at himself or herself and the future. Older adults go through tremendous losses as they grow older. These losses can be imagined, possible, and real. Imagined losses exist only in a person's imagination; for example, when a person thinks someone doesn't like them or care for them anymore when this isn't really true. An example of a possible loss is when a person goes through a number of medical tests and is told there is a possibility that he or she may be ill. A real loss is an actual loss of health as with a severe disease like cancer, or a loss of a spouse to death. The solution to a real loss is to let the grieving process begin. You can help a person cope with an imagined loss by encouraging him or her to try to let it go. A possible loss is the most difficult to deal with. When a loss is threatened, it is impossible to let it go until there is some clarification on what the loss really will entail, and whether or not it will become real.

You can help older adults to cope with these types of less severe cases of depression, first of all by praying with them and for them for the virtue of hope. Determine which type of loss is being experienced. Allow the person to go through a grieving process and help them to face the loss through developing a proper perspective on the loss.

It is never appropriate to belittle another person's loss or compare it to the loss someone else has experienced. You should never tell a person to "snap out of it." None of these approaches show respect for the person or the pain being suffered. Rather, it is more helpful to remind the older adult of all of the blessings in his or her life. Contradict negative statements by the person with positive ones. Help the person to revel in small daily pleasures. Pray together out loud, asking the Holy Spirit to heal the anxiety the person is facing. Above all cultivate a spirit of joy and God's presence. Share this prayer of St. Francis de Sales:

Do not fear what may happen tomorrow.

The same loving Father who cares for you today, will care for you tomorrow and every day.

Either he will shield you from suffering, or he will give you unfailing strength to bear it.

Be at peace then, and put aside all anxious thoughts and imaginings.

Older Adults and Painful Memories

There is an old saying, "An idle mind is a devil's workshop." There is a tendency for some people, as they grow older, to allow the skeletons of painful memories of the past to control their lives. Some older adults carry deep emotional wounds that have never been healed. Carrying these hurts without reconciling them and letting them go can damage one's spiritual, emotional, and physical health.

Those who carry around past hurts often fail to recognize God as the loving Father who is very willing to offer his forgiveness. When hurts are not healed, it is very difficult to recognize Jesus in others and to be Jesus for others. Pastoral caregivers can offer the following helps to older adults who suffer from painful memories:

- Allow the person to admit to his or her hurt. This is one of the first steps toward healing.
- Allow the person to share the hurt with you. Sharing the hurt can be a great relief as the person now brings the pain outward rather than inward. Encourage the person to seek reconciliation in the sacrament of penance.
- Allow the person to embrace the hurt. Jesus says, "Pick up your cross daily and follow me." Embracing the hurt in a constructive way can help the person see the hurt as his or her participation in the redemptive work of Christ. As the hurt is embraced, both self-forgiveness and the forgiveness of the other is able to then logically follow.

For Christians, Jesus is healer *par excellence.* In the gospels, Jesus does not answer the question about why people suffer. Rather, Jesus simply heals the physically, spiritually, and emotionally wounded with a touch, a word, or a prayer. As a pastoral caregiver, you too must send those who are hurting to Jesus. Pray for the person's needs. Pray with the person. And encourage the person to pray for himself or herself, to embrace past hurts, and then let them go to the healing work of Jesus.

Older Adults With Alzheimer's Disease

Alzheimer's disease is a neurological disorder that results in the gradual and progressive loss of brain cells. The disease causes memory loss, which eventually disables the person from performing even the simplest tasks like eating and bathing. Alzheimer's affects a person's speech and personality. He or she may be unable to follow directions, may get lost easily, and may experience severe mood swings. The cause of Alzheimer's is not known and currently there is no cure for the disease.

As a pastoral caregiver you may encounter some form Alzheimer's in an older adult you are visiting. As a person with Alzheimer's may have trouble remembering, use memory aids with him or her. Place familiar religious pictures or statues near the person. Say the same prayers or read the same psalms at each visit. The person's mood and recall ability may change from visit to visit. Be patient with these swings. Remain positive and reassuring.

Speak slowly and softly. Listen attentively to the person and try to understand his or her reality. Do not be disappointed if the person does not recognize you or forgets why you are there. Instead, continue to offer your support, understanding, and prayers. Here are a summary of responses for dealing with the challenging behaviors of Alzheimer's disease:

- Stay calm and understanding.
- Look for reasons for each behavior.
- Do not argue or try to convince.
- Explore various solutions.
- Use memory aids.
- Talk to others about the situation.
- Be patient and flexible.
- Respond to the emotion, not the behavior.
- Acknowledge requests and respond to them.
- Find other outlets for an inappropriate behavior.
- Try not to take behaviors personally.
- Find time for yourself.

Older Adults and Assisted Living

Selecting a long term or short term facility for assisted living is one of the most difficult decisions an older adult and his or her family members will have to make. This decision may have to be made quickly, as a person may have a sudden health problem that requires special and immediate care. Finding the right kind of services requires the examination of many issues and facts. Remember, as a pastoral caregiver you are only in an advisory position. The person you are caring for and his or her primary caregiver must be involved in all facets of making this important decision. However, you can be of great help by acquainting yourself with all facets of this decision and assisting the person and his or her family appropriately by answering or obtaining answers to questions they may have.

In exploring solutions to the need for assisted living, the possibility of using a home care or community-based care provider should be explored first. Among these services are home health care, respite care, adult day care centers, foster care, residential care in a board-and-care home, retirement communities, and hospice care.

If the family proceeds in seeking assisted living for an older adult, help them to take the process one step at a time. For example, this basic information can help: When seeking a placement, call and ask for a tour of the facility. Make sure to talk to the residents. Know that if the older adult you are advising is a Medicare or Medicaid beneficiary who is applying to a facility covered by one of those plans, it is unlawful for the facility to require a cash deposit. The facility may request that the beneficiary pay co-insurance amounts or other charges for which a beneficiary is liable. Those charges must be paid only as they become due, not before. If a person is not covered by Medicare or Medicaid, the facility may ask for a cash deposit before admission.

There are several questions you should ask as you evaluate a care facility for older adults. For example:

- Is the facility licensed to provide the care needed?
- What are the admissions requirements?
- Does the facility have vacancies?

- What type of payment does the facility accept (Medicare, Medicaid, private insurance, etc.)?
- What are additional costs besides the basic rate (e.g., laundry, field trips, medications, toiletries)?
- What type of social program does the facility offer?
- Is the facility associated with a church?
- What types of religious services or communal prayer are offered?
- Is the food made at the facility or is it prepared elsewhere?
- How much variety is there on the menu?
- How does the food appear?
- Are snacks between meals available?
- Are menus for special diets (e.g., diabetics) available?
- How approachable are staff members?
- What are the types of staffing positions?
- What are the qualifications of each staff position?
- What is the demeanor of the residents (neat, clean, happy)?
- Are the residents dressed for the time of day and season of the year?

- Are there unpleasant odors?
- Do noise levels coincide with the activities that are going on?
- Is there a separate unit for residents with dementia or Alzheimer's disease?
- Is there a residents' council where residents can voice their opinions?
- Does the residents' council impact facility policy?
- How easily are residents able to have access to their own doctor?
- What is the cooperation between the facility and a resident's HMO?
- What therapy services are available at the facility (e.g., speech, language, motor skills)?

Even after a family selects an assisted living facility the period of adjustment for everyone concerned will likely be difficult. It is only natural to have feelings like "I let my mother down," or "I should be able to take care of my father," when placing a loved one in an assisted living facility. However, a professionally run facility that treats its residents with dignity and respect can feel like home to its residents.

Families must stay involved with most decisions made at the facility on behalf of a loved one. For example, a trust fund can be set up at a local bank in the name of the resident to invest his or her money and pay all the bills. Family members should attend regular meetings with staff and discuss the staff's individual care plan for their relative (including a naming of all medications given to a person and their side effects). A living will should be arranged and family members should be granted durable power of attorney. Visits are the best way to remain involved. Family members—and you as a pastoral caregiver—should visit with the person living at the assisted care facility as much as possible, including during drop-in times and at mealtimes. The more everyone stays involved the better.

Older Adults and Subsidized Housing

Though there is usually a long waiting list, there are affordable housing apartments available to persons sixty-two years of age and older. The rents are subsidized by Section 8 funding from the federal government. Section 8 housing is primarily made up of one bedroom apartments with a kitchen, living room, and a bathroom specially built for the needs of older adults. There are usually two large closets in the apartments and a locked storage area for large items. These one bedroom apartments are designed for occupancy by one or two persons. There may also be a few two bedroom apartments. All units are built for independent living. The tenant is responsible for the normal upkeep of the apartment and for maintaining his or her personal property and furnishings within the apartment. Maintenance staff is available to correct major mechanical problems within the unit.

Because of the Housing Urban and Development (HUD) subsidy, a tenant's rent is based on 30 percent of the tenant's adjusted annual income (gross income minus applicable medical expenses). This results in the tenant paying less than 30 percent of his or her adjusted income for rent on a monthly basis. A national HUD information telephone number is included on page 165 of the Resource section.

Another housing option for older adults that has recently become more prevalent is residential care homes. These facilities are sometimes called personal care homes or shelter homes for older adults. They usually provide part-time nursing care, three meals a day, assistance for bathing and dressing, housekeeping services, transportation to the doctor and dentist, and a twenty-four-hour semi-professional trained staff. Also, each resident has an emergency call button to summon help.

In residential care homes the older adult may choose an individual room, suite, studio apartment, or even a one or two bedroom villa. The residents supply their own home furnishings. The residents are able to come together for meals and activities and enjoy the companionship of other older adults. This type of arrangement allows an individual as much independence as he or she wants or needs, but provides help with meals and personal care. These facilities can be very expensive and it is wise to have a lawyer read over the housing agreement before a contract is signed.

"That Child Will Take Care of You"

Ginny and Tom are a married couple in their late forties who live comfortably in a small city in western Pennsylvania. Ginny's mother Bertha lived with the couple for the entire duration of their marriage. The following is a true account of how Ginny and Tom faced and ultimately postponed the decision of moving Bertha to an assisted care facility.

Bertha suffered a variety of debilitating ailments throughout her life. However, after her husband died she didn't worry about who would take care of her. Bertha often relates a tale of the time when she was pregnant with Ginny at the hearty age of forty-two. Bertha felt depressed because she thought some of her lady friends were making fun of her condition. "Don't let them bother you, Bertha," one friend remarked. "You're having that child for a reason. Mark my words, that child will take care of you!"

And so it was practically pre-ordained that Ginny would care for her mother in Bertha's later years.

Throughout their years of marriage, Tom and Ginny, both professionals, worked outside the home while Bertha did household chores like cooking, cleaning, and the laundry. For the most part, the arrangement worked well. Each family member felt useful and needed in the home. As Bertha aged, Ginny and Tom took over the vacuuming or whatever chores Bertha felt she could no longer perform in the house. But just after Bertha turned eighty-seven, her body started to betray her in many critical ways. Over the next few months she had less and less energy. She slept a lot. She became more forgetful; for example, she had trouble remembering whether she had something simmering on the electric range. The arthritis pain in her back became more pronounced. She needed the aid of a walker to get around. Worse yet Bertha began experiencing quick blackouts which caused her to lose her balance and fall. Thankfully, none of these falls resulted in more than cuts, scrapes, and bruises. But taken all together, the symptoms were alarming.

Early one December morning Ginny and Tom were abruptly awakened by the sound of a body rolling down the staircase and landing with a heavy thud. Bertha was disoriented when reached seconds later, but she shook off the cobwebs after a few minutes and demanded that someone help her up. Once on her feet she set off to the kitchen announcing that she was going to make the coffee. Nothing was broken except a post from the oak stair railing! This episode ended fortunately, but Tom and Ginny realized it was just the beginning of much more serious problems.

For years Ginny had told her mother that when she could no longer climb the stairs, the dining room could easily be converted into a bedroom. Shortly after Tom and Ginny set about to make the change.

They expected a fight from Bertha when Tom began dismantling the dining room table. Instead, the still-shaken octogenarian decided that the change would be acceptable "for a while." Bertha's bed was outfitted with a railing, a chest-of-drawers filled with some of her favorite outfits was brought downstairs, and fabric curtains hung in the opening allowed for some privacy. From this base, Bertha could do all she needed to care for herself while

Ginny and Tom were at work. Yet Bertha's health continued to erode. When Ginny's sister, Sister Teresa, visited at Christmas, she met for a serious talk with the third sibling, older brother Damian, who also lived in town. Not wanting to upset Ginny or their mother, the two siblings agreed that all should recognize that Bertha needed more care than she was getting at home.

Damian had already taken the time to visit the diocesan-sponsored nursing home Bertha expressed interest in many years before. He talked to the director of placement, learned some of the family's responsibilities, and picked up brochures and an application for admittance. That same day he sat down with Ginny and their mom to discuss what he had learned. He also informed them the home had fifteen open beds, several in lovely private rooms. Thus, the ground-work was laid when Sister Teresa came home for the holiday.

Ginny, Tom, and Teresa visited the nursing home a few days before Christmas. They walked the halls, stopped in the chapel, visited with the residents in the dining room, and toured one of the private rooms. The room, furnished with a hospital bed, desk, easy-chair, and a sink, also had a good sized closet and a shared bath. Each floor had a large walk-in bath area which could accommodate a wheelchair. Ginny and Teresa were pleased by what they saw, and even a little excited for their mother's opportunity to be cared for in such a well-kept, hospitable facility. Before they left, they talked to the placement director and financial aid director. The discussions were light and helpful, but Ginny began to have some reservations. It seemed to her that the whole process of placing their beloved mother in the nursing home was too smooth and easy.

When they got home, they talked with Bertha about all they had seen and learned. Bertha herself was impressed, but also somewhat apprehensive about "leaving home." However, in the days immediately after, all of the private rooms became filled. Ginny did not believe her mother needed hospital-style care so she made the decision that her mother could wait until one of the nice private rooms became available again. The director of placement agreed this seemed to be a sensible position under the circumstances.

A day or so later, a small miracle happened. Bertha had an appointment with her podiatrist for an open wound that refused to heal. The doctor suggested regular wound dressing by a home health care professional might encourage the healing. A home health care nurse decided a nurse specifically trained in skin care should take a look at the offending foot, then discuss care options with her doctor. As a result Bertha had an extra visitor those weeks. Another time, Ginny asked if physical therapy was available to assist her mother with simple tasks like getting out of a chair or putting up the footrest on her reclining chair. As a result, a physical therapist was dispatched to the house.

It turned out that with home health care and its many complementary services (including a social worker who helped with Bertha's financial needs and set up a life-line monitoring system for her), Bertha was able to remain at Ginny and Tom's home even after a private room opened up at the facility. Through home health care Bertha enjoyed regular visits with caring, highly-qualified nurses. At one point the visits were daily, including weekends.

The social worker was also helpful to Ginny and Tom. She explained that when Bertha signed her assets over to the nursing home that the money would be used for her care. But also that the money would probably all be consumed in ten months. After that, Medicaid guaranteed Bertha's continued nursing care, but that care would not necessarily be provided in the home of her choice. She might, instead, be sent to a less-costly personal care home, or a state-supported nursing home. Such homes in Bertha's local area were rated as good care facilities, but Bertha might be deprived of the Catholic atmosphere she longed for in her final years.

Ginny discussed the social worker's comments with her mother, Tom, and later by phone with her brother and sister. Ginny and her mother agreed that all of Bertha's assets should be put to use for her own care—preferably at Tom and Ginny's home.

Today, Bertha is still able to function in her own home, and she can still feel useful within her family.

Many days she has dinner ready when Ginny and Tom get home from work. She helps to fold the laundry. She keeps the kitchen tidy. Most importantly, she enjoys the love that is generated within a family—her family.

Later, when her problems advance beyond the kind that the family and the many services of home health care can handle, Bertha will use her money for the specialized care of a nursing home.

The situation is not a perfect one for everyone involved because life is not perfect. Occasionally tempers flare and son Damian would still like to see his mother's needs met in the more constant environment of a nursing home. But for now, Bertha is settled in her daughter's home, a place she has called her home for nearly twenty years.

Older Adults and Home Health Care

Most older adults prefer to remain in their own homes as long as they are able. Generally it costs more to live in a long-term care facility than it does to stay at home. One strategy for paying for "home health care" is to borrow against the cash value of the older adult's life insurance policy. Some older adults take out a reverse mortgage to tap the equity in their homes.

Several types of services are provided by home health care agencies. Included in these are:

- *Personal care services.* These services include minor household repairs, cleaning, and yard work. Also, home health aids offer non-medical services such as bathing, dressing, cooking, cleaning, laundry, and running errands.

- *Home maintenance and repair.* Besides basic upkeep, this service includes making a home handicap accessible and secure. Often these improvements can be paid for on a sliding scale according to an individual's income or with low interest loans that do not have to be repaid until a homeowner sells or leaves the home.

- *Meal services.* Agencies like "Meals on Wheels" provide a nutritionally balanced meal five or more days a week to those who cannot do their own grocery shopping or prepare meals. (If possible an older adult may have at least one meal a day at a local senior citizen center where he or she can enjoy camaraderie and companionship.)

- *Friendly visitors.* "Friendly" visitors make regular visits to homebound older adults. The companionship can alleviate loneliness and isolation. They may just talk and reminisce, read, or help with writing letters. These visitors do many of the same things of a church-sponsored pastoral caregiver.

- *Telephone reassurance.* Some agencies make sure that the person who lives alone receives a call during the day. The phone call is usually at a predetermined time. If the contact is not made the caller alerts a neighbor or relative to check on the older adult. If no one is available to check, an emergency service is dispatched.

- *Senior citizen centers.* Centers are places where older adults come together to enjoy each other's company. Senior citizen centers usually provide nutritional, social, and educational services based on the needs and interests of the older adult clientele.
- *Transportation.* Most communities have a transportation service that provides transportation for older adults to medical appointments, the physical therapist, the grocery store, or the local senior citizen's center. Most services are free or charged on a sliding scale based on the person's income.

Every community has several resources and agencies that allow more and more people to remain at home.

To help offer information about home health care options, first identify the type of services needed. Call a local senior citizen's center, an Area Agency on Aging (AAA), the local Social Security office, or any of the toll free numbers in the Human Services Directory of the Resource section (pages 167-179). You will be referred to the appropriate state or local information and resource referral source for a variety of services, including:

home-delivered meals, transportation, legal assistance, affordable housing, adult day care, social and recreational activities, senior center programs, and the nursing-home ombudsman.

Older Adults and Abuse

Unfortunately abuse of older adults is a reality. Abuse may take place in a care facility or even in a person's own home at the hands of a primary caregiver. If you are aware of abuse, you should contact the Area Agency on Aging in your area for information on the law and due process in your state.

The following signs are intended for you to recognize older adult abuse. The older person may:

- have bruises, broken bones, abrasions to both arms or wrists indicating that they may have been restrained;
- appear malnourished or dehydrated;
- have glasses or dentures missing;
- be under or over medicated;
- be confused, anxious, withdrawn, timid, or depressed.

Also, the older person's primary caregiver may:

- fail to provide medication or proper medical care;
- fail to keep the person properly dressed or cleaned;
- display violent behavior or excessive anger;
- have a history of personal problems;
- give conflicting stories about what is happening to the older person.

Also financial exploitation is a form of abuse itself. Signs of potential exploitation are the sudden closing of bank accounts or large withdrawals, abrupt changes in a person's will, signs of poverty in spite of sufficient resources, a caregiver's new-found wealth, or a sudden transfer of property.

Remember, if you are aware of possible abuse, contact your pastor, a parish staff person, and/or another authority. Your reporting of this problem can be handled confidentially.

Older Adults and Difficult Medical Decisions

While every person has the right to make his or her own decisions on the type and intensity of medical care they wish to receive, as a pastoral caregiver you may be asked for your advice on certain procedures. As a representative of the church, your responses should be to help the person and the family understand principles which emphasize a consistent life ethic from conception to death.

In making medical decisions it is important to distinguish between proportionate and disproportionate treatments. Proportionate treatments are acceptable means that offer the person a reasonable hope of improved health without imposing excessive burdens upon the person, family, or community. Disproportionate treatments are non-acceptable means as they impose excessive physical, emotional, financial, or spiritual hardships on the person, family, or community. Medical decisions are to be made by assessing the hope of benefit in relationship to the burdens encountered.

The most difficult medical decisions to be made generally occur near the end of life. A person may choose to use, withhold, or withdraw life-sustaining procedures. In making these determinations, the person must decide if the burdens of the treatment outweigh the benefits hoped to be gained. If the decision is made to not use or withdraw life support systems, the proportionate treatment that would be offered would be care, compassion, and keeping the patient free from pain. The intention in this example is to accept and allow the incurable condition to progress naturally to death rather than prolonging the burden of the dying process. It would be morally wrong to discontinue nutrition and hydration when they are within the realm of ordinary means. By accepting the inevitability of death, the person ultimately acknowledges his or her humanity and recognizes his or her belief in the resurrection of Christ and eternal life.

Allowing a person to die when nothing more can be done medically is different from a deliberate act of omission intended to kill the patient as in the act of euthanasia or physician assisted suicide. Suicide is a deliberate decision by an individual about how and when he or she wants to die. Assisted suicide is the involvement of another person cooperating with and assisting in the person's decision to die. Euthanasia is the practice of killing individuals who are sick or injured without their consent for reasons of mercy.

As euthanasia and assisted suicide gain greater acceptance in society at large, a common view is that if pain can be alleviated, the person has the right to control his or her time of death. A common refrain is, "I would not want to be kept alive that way," in reference to the need for certain medical aids. Other dying people say, "I want to get it over with." Sometimes these sentiments are expressed by the person only to check and see if anyone really cares whether or not he or she lives. Or, the person may be lacking real alternatives due to inadequate medical treatment, improper long-term care, or self-esteem. Additionally, the person may be clinically depressed which properly treated may alter his or her judgment. Pastoral caregivers must share with the person the message that life is God's gift and that he or she is entrusted to be a proper steward of that gift. Sometimes this stewardship involves sharing in the redemptive suffering of Jesus Christ. As a pastoral caregiver, you should assure the person that he or she has your compassion, care, companionship, and support.

There is much confusion and anxiety today on moral questions surrounding death and dying. One of the most challenging issues is physician assisted suicide. In 1997 the United States Supreme Court ruled that physician assisted suicide is a constitutionally protected right of the patient and the physician. This ruling left the decision to ban assisted suicide up to individual states.

As a pastoral caregiver you have the solemn obligation to provide the dying person with realistic and compassionate care. Assisted suicide is *not* realistic and compassionate care. In fact the literal meaning of compassion is "to suffer with." We must always keep in mind that we are created in God's image and likeness and are stewards of God's gift of life. Death is not the end. In the depths of our hearts, the voice of God reiterates the same ageless message: "Thou shall not kill." Suicide is always morally wrong. Concurring with someone's intention to commit suicide and cooperate in the process can never be condoned and must be vehemently protested as strongly as you are able.

Rite of Distributing Holy Communion Outside Mass

The following rite is taken from Pastoral Care of the Sick: Rite of Anointing and Viaticum. *This rite is to be used chiefly when Mass is not celebrated or when communion is not distributed at scheduled times. The purpose is that the people will be nourished by the Word of God. By hearing God's word, they can learn that the marvels it proclaims reach their climax in the paschal mystery of which the Mass is a sacramental memorial and in which they share communion.*

This rite is appropriate to use with older adults who are homebound or who live in a nursing home setting. You may wish to have a standing crucifix, a cloth napkin, and a candle on a central table. When preparations are complete, all stand (if able) for the greeting.

Greeting

The pastoral caregiver greets those present with these or similar words:

> Brothers and sisters, the Lord invites us (you) to his table to share in the body of Christ: bless him for his goodness.
> **R:** Blessed be God forever.

Or:

> The peace of the Lord be with you.
> **R:** And also with you.

Penitential Rite

After the greeting, the pastoral caregiver leads the penitential rite.

> My brothers and sisters, to prepare ourselves for this celebration, let us call to mind our sins.

A pause for silent reflection follows before one of the following rites is used.

> Lord Jesus, you heal the sick,
> Lord have mercy.
> **R:** Lord have mercy.

Lord Jesus you forgive sinners,
Christ have mercy.
R: Christ have mercy.
Lord Jesus you gave us yourself to heal us
and bring us strength,
Lord have mercy.
R: Lord have mercy.

Or:

All: I confess to almighty God
and to you, my brothers and sisters,
that I have sinned through my own fault
in my thoughts and in my words,
in what I have done,
and in what I have failed to do;
and I ask blessed Mary, ever virgin,
all the angels and saints,
and you, my brothers and sisters,
to pray for me to the Lord our God.

_The minister concludes the penitential rite with
the following text:_

May almighty God have mercy on us,
forgive us our sins,

and bring us to everlasting life.
R: Amen

Scripture Reading

*The liturgy of the word now takes place as at
Mass. Texts are chosen for the occasion either
from the Mass of the day or from the votive
Masses of the Holy Eucharist or the Precious
Blood (see Lectionary). There may be one or more
readings, the first being followed by a psalm,
song, or by a period of silent prayer. The liturgy
of the word concludes with a sharing of the general intercessions.*

Communion Rite

*The pastoral caregiver then introduces the Lord's
Prayer in these or similar words.*

Let us pray with confidence to the Father in
the words our Savior gave us:
Our Father . . .

*The minister genuflects. Taking the host, he or she
raises it slightly over the vessel or pyx and faces
the people, and says:*

This is the Lamb of God
who takes away the sins of the world.
Happy are those who are called to his supper.
R: Lord, I am not worthy to receive you,
but only say the word and I shall be
healed.

_The pastoral caregiver goes to the communicants,
takes a host for each one, raises it slightly, and
says:_

The body of Christ.
R: Amen

_After communion, a period of silence may be
observed, or a psalm or song of praise may be
sung._

Concluding Rite

The pastoral caregiver leads the concluding prayer.
Let us pray:
Lord, Jesus Christ,
you gave us the eucharist
as the memorial of your suffering and death.
May our worship of this sacrament of your
body and blood

help us to experience the salvation you won
for us
and the peace of the kingdom
where you live with the Father and the Holy
Spirit,
one God, forever and ever.
R: Amen

*The pastoral caregiver invokes God's blessing
and, crossing himself or herself, says one of the
following.*

May the Lord bless us,
protect us from all evil
and bring us to everlasting life.

Or:

May the almighty and merciful God bless us
and protect us,
the Father and the Son, + and the Holy Spirit.
R: Amen

Prayer Service

The following selection is from the Pastoral Care
of the Sick: Rite of Anointing and Viaticum. *It is*

*approved by the Apostolic See. Please note that
other readings and psalms may be found in the*
Pastoral Care of the Sick. *It may be used in total
or as part of a prayer service at a nursing home,
hospital, or in someone's home.*

Scripture Reading

*The word of God is proclaimed by one of those
present or by the pastoral caregiver. One of the
following readings or another taken from* Pastoral
Care of the Sick *may be used:*

A reading from the Acts of the Apostles (3:1-10).

Once, when Peter and John were going up to the
temple for prayer at the three o'clock hour, a man
crippled from birth was being carried in. They
would bring him every day and put him at the temple gate called "the Beautiful" to beg from the people as they entered. When he saw Peter and John on
their way in, he begged them for alms. Peter fixed
his gaze on the man; so did John. "Look at us!"
Peter said. The cripple gave them his whole attention, hoping to get something. Then Peter said: "I
have neither silver nor gold, but what I have I give
you! In the name of Jesus Christ the Nazorean,

walk!" Then Peter took him by the right hand and pulled him up. Immediately the beggar's feet and ankles became strong; he jumped up, stood for a moment, then began to walk around. He went into the temple with them—walking, jumping about, and praising God. When the people saw him moving and giving praise to God, they recognized him as that beggar who used to sit at the Beautiful Gate of the temple. They were struck with astonishment— utterly stupefied at what had happened to him.

The Word of the Lord.

Or:

A reading from the holy gospel according to Matthew (8:14-17).

Jesus entered Peter's house and found Peter's mother-in-law in bed with a fever. He took her by the hand and the fever left her. She got up at once and began to wait on him.

As evening drew on, they brought him many who were possessed. He expelled the spirits by a simple command and cured all who were afflicted, thereby fulfilling what had been said through Isaiah the prophet:

"It was our infirmities he bore,
   our sufferings he endured."
The gospel of the Lord.

Psalm Response

A brief period of silence may be observed after the scripture reading. One of the following psalms may be used as a response.

Psalm 102

R: O Lord, hear my prayer,
   and let my cry come to you.

O Lord, hear my prayer,
   and let my cry come to you.
Hide not your face from me
   in the day of my distress.
Incline your ear to me;
   in the day when I call, answer me
   speedily.
R: O Lord, hear my prayer,
   and let my cry come to you.

He has broken down my strength in the way;
   he has cut short my days.

I say: O my God,
Take me not hence in the midst of my days;
    through all generations your years
    endure.
R: O Lord, hear my prayer,
    and let my cry come to you.

Let this be written for the generation to come,
    and let his future creatures praise the
    Lord:
"The Lord looked down from his holy height,
    from heaven he beheld the earth,
To hear the groaning of the prisoners,
    to release those doomed to die."
R: O Lord, hear my prayer,
    and let my cry come to you.

Or:

Psalm 27

    R: The Lord is my light and my salvation.

The Lord is my light and my salvation;
    whom should I fear?
The Lord is my life's refuge;
    of whom should I be afraid?

R: The Lord is my light and my salvation.

One thing I ask of the Lord;
   this I seek:
To dwell in the house of the Lord
   all the days of my life,
That I may gaze on the loveliness of the Lord
   and contemplate his temple.
R: The Lord is my light and my salvation.

For he will hide me in his abode
   in the day of trouble;
He will conceal me in the shelter of his tent,
   he will set me high upon a rock.
R: The Lord is my light and my salvation.

More Psalms

The psalms are wonderful "song prayers," full of meaning when you pray with others. The following psalms or others offered in Pastoral Care of the Sick *may be used as part of a prayer service or simply as shared prayer with an older adult you are visiting with.*

Psalm 23   The Lord Is My Shepherd
Psalm 25   Prayer for Guidance and Help
Psalm 34   God, Our Protector
Psalm 62   Trust in God Alone
Psalm 71   Prayer in Time of Old Age
Psalm 91   Security Under God's Protection
Psalm 104 Praise of God as Creator
Psalm 138 Hymn of a Grateful Heart

Reflection

The pastoral caregiver may then give a brief explanation of the reading, applying it to the needs of the sick person and those who are looking after him or her.

The Lord's Prayer

The pastoral caregiver introduces the Lord's Prayer in these or similar words:

Now let us offer together the prayer our Lord Jesus Christ taught us.

All: Our Father . . .

Concluding Prayer

The pastoral caregiver says a concluding prayer. One of the following may be used:

Let us pray.
     Father,
     your Son accepted our sufferings
     to teach us the virtue of patience in human illness.

Hear the prayers we offer for our sick
brother/sister.
May all who suffer pain, illness, or disease
realize that they have been chosen to be saints
and know that they are joined to Christ
in his suffering for the salvation of the world.

We ask this through Christ our Lord. Amen.
Or:
Let us pray.
All-powerful and ever-living God,
the lasting health of all who believe in you,
hear us as we ask your loving help for the sick;
restore their health,
that they may again offer joyful thanks in
your Church.

Grant this through Christ our Lord. Amen.
Or:
Let us pray.
All-powerful and ever-living God.
We find security in your forgiveness.
Give us serenity and peace of mind;
may we rejoice in your gifts of kindness
and use them always for your glory and our
good.

We ask this in the name of Jesus the Lord.
Amen.

Blessing

The minister pastoral caregiver may give a blessing. One of the following may be used.

All praise and glory is yours, Lord our God,
for you have called us to serve you in love.
Bless N.
so that he / she may bear this illness
in union with your Son's obedient suffering.
Restore him / her to health,
and lead him / her to glory.

We ask this through Christ our Lord. Amen.
Or:
For an elderly person
All praise and glory are yours, Lord our God,
for you have called us to serve you in love.
Bless all who have grown old in your love
and give N. strength and courage
to continue to follow Jesus your Son.

We ask this through Christ our Lord. Amen.

Stations of the Cross

The fifteen meditations on the passion, death, and resurrection of Jesus are based on the traditional Stations of the Cross, a popular prayer noted by stations on the walls of most Catholic churches. To pray the stations in a retirement home or other assisted living facility simply read a meditation, pause for personal reflection, read another, and so on. An Our Father, Hail Mary, or Glory Be may be added after each one. Slides of the particular stations can be shown on a screen or blank wall as the meditation is read.

Opening Prayer

Let us pray that these meditations on the Lord's passion, death, and resurrection will help us to open our hearts and help us to live according to God's will. We ask this in the name of Christ our Lord. Amen.

We adore you, O Christ, and we praise you.
R: Because by your holy cross you have redeemed the world.

1. Jesus Is Condemned to Death

Jesus stands alone before Pilate, scourged, and crowned with thorns. He is told how he will die. We may not have the blessing to know the place, time, or circumstances of our death. We do know that we are destined to die from the moment we are conceived. In this knowledge, we need to hand ourselves over to Jesus. God knows what is best for us. Let us pray that we can discover a deeper peace and acceptance of all our difficulties.

We adore you, O Christ, and we praise you.

R: Because by your holy cross you have redeemed the world.

2. Jesus Carries His Cross

By accepting our daily crosses, we share in the suffering of Jesus. Crosses have been given to each of us. We did not choose these crosses for ourselves. Our crosses are not to punish us, but refine us. We pray that we may learn the wisdom of the triumph of the cross and that we may carry our crosses patiently and lovingly. We asks this in Jesus' name.

We adore you, O Christ, and we praise you.

R: Because by your holy cross you have redeemed the world.

3. Jesus Falls Under the Weight of the Cross

We sometimes forget to let God guide our lives. We forget to let God work through us. Instead, we call attention to ourselves. May we who fall from weakness find the strength to get up and keep going as Christ did as he walked along the way.

We adore you, O Christ, and we praise you.

R: Because by your holy cross you have redeemed the world.

4. Jesus Meets His Mother

Imagine what the Blessed Mother felt when she saw the beaten, weak body of her Son. Mary may have run away from this heart-piercing experience, but she stayed and served as a model for all Christians. Mary sees our pain and is an affirming companion for all who suffer. Let us pray that we accept our own crosses and open our hearts to help others in their pain.

We adore you, O Christ, and we praise you.

R: Because by your holy cross you have redeemed the world.

5. Simon of Cyrene Helps Jesus Carry His Cross

Jesus' strength is gone. He can no longer bear the cross alone. Jesus is encouraged by the helping hand of Simon, another human being. Help us, O Lord, to do more than just sit and watch. Help us to be doers. Make us ready and willing to help our neighbors. Let us be the hands and heart for those who cannot find love and care in our world.

We adore you, O Christ, and we praise you.

R: Because by your holy cross you have redeemed the world.

6. Veronica Wipes the Face of Jesus

Jesus' face is bathed in sweat and blood. Veronica steps forward, presents her veil, and wipes the face of Jesus. Lord, help us to regard every opportunity for kindness as an act that will last for eternity, as Jesus' image remained on the sacred cloth.

We adore you, O Christ, and we praise you.

R: Because by your holy cross you have redeemed the world.

7. Jesus Falls a Second Time

Jesus finds it very hard to get up after he falls a second time. There are so many things that try to keep us down. We don't understand all of them. Father, give us the strength to get up again as Jesus did. We ask this in his name.

We adore you, O Christ, and we praise you.

R: Because by your holy cross you have redeemed the world.

8. Jesus Meets the Women of Jerusalem

The sight of Jesus leads those along the way to turn away and cry. Jesus stops for a moment and offers comfort to the women who cry for him. Jesus tells them to pray for themselves. When we are in pain, how do we keep from focusing on our own needs and try instead to make those around us feel better? Let us pray that we might think more of others than ourselves.

We adore you, O Christ, and we praise you.

R: Because by your holy cross you have redeemed the world.

9. Jesus Falls a Third Time

We know that in loving fidelity to his Father's will and out of compassion for each of us, Jesus accepts the heavy burden of the cross. We are called to accept our own crosses. We know how hard it is to get up some mornings to face the challenges that await us. We may wonder, "What good am I to anyone?" Instead let us join Jesus in the carrying of our crosses. Let us not be discouraged with our human frailty and sinfulness, no matter how many times we fall. Help us, Lord, to go forward in your path of love.

We adore you, O Christ, and we praise you.
R: Because by your holy cross you have redeemed the world.

10. Jesus Is Stripped of His Garments

The soldiers rip off Jesus' cloak. He is stripped of every shred of human dignity. Let us never forget that some day we will stand naked before our almighty and loving God. Without God's help we are nothing. Help us to empty ourselves of our sin and selfishness and not even flinch when our own self-dignity is stripped away by illness or aging. May we be poor in spirit so that God's Spirit can be rich in us.

We adore you, O Christ, and we praise you.
R: Because by your holy cross you have
redeemed the world.

11. Jesus Is Nailed to the Cross

Jesus' arms are stretched. The executioners
hold his hand and wrist against the wood and press
the nail until it stabs his flesh. Then with heavy
hammer blows they drive the nails through. Jesus
did not let out a cry or even a whimper. Instead he
went along with this most terrifying pain. Let us
pray that God will be with us when we must experience physical and mental torment. Help us to
realize that through our daily crosses we complete
the suffering of Christ on this earth.

We adore you, O Christ, and we praise you.
R: Because by your holy cross you have
redeemed the world.

12. Jesus Dies

As Jesus hangs on the cross dying, the multi-
tudes see their own efforts and dreams collapse.
Jesus even cries out in doubt to his Father. But in
the end Jesus dies the way he has lived . . . with
total trust in his Father's love. Because of his death,

the world is now redeemed. Let us pray that we might be able to offer our own death to our heavenly Father. Let us pray that at the time of death we will be comforted by our loving Lord.

We adore you, O Christ, and we praise you.

R: Because by your holy cross you have redeemed the world.

13. Jesus Is Taken Down From the Cross

The commotion is over. Life around Jerusalem begins to return to normal. Meanwhile Jesus' body is taken down from the cross. Imagine Jesus' mother cradling the lifeless body of her Son in her arms. Lord, help us to accept the parting that comes with death, as with friends and family who move or are far away. Pray for us, Lord, at the hour of our own deaths.

We adore you, O Christ, and we praise you.

R: Because by your holy cross you have redeemed the world.

14. Jesus Is Laid in the Tomb

Joseph of Arimathea takes the body of Jesus and lays it in a tomb cut out of rock. He rolls a large stone in front of the tomb and sadly goes home. Jesus is buried. The tomb was borrowed, just as Jesus borrowed Peter's boat from which to preach, just as Jesus borrowed the colt on which he entered Jerusalem. Jesus borrows us to be his hands and voice to the world today. When Jesus finishes with us he will call us home to be with him.

We adore you, O Christ, and we praise you.

R: Because by your holy cross you have redeemed the world.

15. Jesus Rises From the Dead

The darkness of the night has given way to the brightness of dawn. The tomb is empty. The God-man again walks the face of the earth. Jesus is risen. All sufferings and tortures are swallowed up in the glory of the resurrection. We too will share in his glory. Let us look to the empty tomb when we feel ourselves closed or confined. Let us go, take up our crosses, and complete the life of Christ by proclaiming the good news that he is risen indeed. May the victory of the resurrection spread its peace and joy throughout our lives.

We adore you, O Christ, and we praise you.

R: Because by your holy cross you have redeemed the world.

Litanies

A litany can be led by a pastoral caregiver with a group or individual and can be used in place of a prayer service. Make sure the participants know the response. When it is time for a response, the pastoral caregiver should raise his or her hand so that all will be cued in. The litany of saints on pages 147-151 is adapted from the Pastoral Care of the Sick.

Litany of Thanksgiving

Leader: O Loving God and Father, we know that you are always with us, even when everything around us passes away. Teach us to bear with patience the infirmities of advancing years. In our growing loneliness, help us to realize that you are always here. For this and all of the following we thank you Lord. For all the days you have given us . . .

R: We thank you O God.

Leader: For all we are yet to receive . . .

R: We thank you O God.

Leader: For this time we enjoy together . . .

R: We thank you O God.

Leader: For the entire communion of saints on heaven and earth . . .

R: We thank you O God.

Leader: For the gift of humility that allows us to appreciate your goodness . . .

R: We thank you O God.

Leader: Let us pray. Heavenly Father, out of love for us you sent your Son, Jesus, into the world so that all might live abundantly. Inspire us to be good servants throughout our whole life span, that we may use our strengths wisely and our talents for your glory. May we always support, console, encourage, and love one another all the days of our lives. We ask this in the name of Jesus Christ our Lord.

R: Amen.

Litany of the Saints

Lord, have mercy.   R: Lord, have mercy.

Christ, have mercy.   R: Christ, have mercy.

Lord, have mercy.   R: Lord, have mercy.

Holy Mary,
Mother of God,   R: pray for us.

Holy angels of God,   R: pray for us.

Abraham, our father
in faith,   R: pray for us.

David, leader
of God's people,   R: pray for us.

All holy patriarchs
and prophets,   R: pray for us.

Saint John the Baptist, R: pray for us.

Saint Joseph,   R: pray for us.

Saint Peter and
Saint Paul,   R: pray for us.

Saint Andrew,	**R:** pray for us.
Saint John,	**R:** pray for us.
Saint Mary Magdalene,	**R:** pray for us.
Saint Stephen,	**R:** pray for us.
Saint Ignatius,	**R:** pray for us.
Saint Lawrence,	**R:** pray for us.
Saint Perpetua and Saint Felicity,	**R:** pray for us.
Saint Agnes,	**R:** pray for us.
Saint Gregory,	**R:** pray for us.
Saint Augustine,	**R:** pray for us.
Saint Athanasius,	**R:** pray for us.
Saint Basil,	**R:** pray for us.
Saint Martin,	**R:** pray for us.
Saint Benedict,	**R:** pray for us.

Saint Francis and Saint Dominic,	**R:** pray for us.
Saint Francis Xavier,	**R:** pray for us.
Saint John Vianney,	**R:** pray for us.
Saint Catherine,	**R:** pray for us.
Saint Teresa,	**R:** pray for us.

Other saints may be included here.

All holy men and women,	**R:** pray for us.
Lord, be merciful.	**R:** Lord, save your people.
From all evil,	**R:** Lord, save your people.
From every sin,	**R:** Lord, save your people.
From Satan's power,	**R:** Lord, save your people.

At the moment of death

From everlasting death,	**R:** Lord, save your people.
On the day of judgment,	**R:** Lord, save your people.
By your coming as man,	**R:** Lord, save your people.
By your suffering and cross,	**R:** Lord, save your people.
By your death and rising to new life,	**R:** Lord, save your people.
By your return in glory to the Father,	**R:** Lord, save your people.
By your gift of the Holy Spirit,	**R:** Lord, save your people.
By your coming again in glory,	**R:** Lord, save your people.

Be merciful to   R: Lord, hear our
us sinners,   prayer.

Jesus, Son of   R: Lord, hear our
the living God,   prayer.

Christ, hear us.   R: Christ, hear us.

Lord Jesus,   R: Lord Jesus, hear
hear our prayer.   our prayer.

Traditional Prayers

The following are some traditional prayers that may be shared between pastoral caregivers and older adults.

Morning Offering

Most holy and adorable Trinity, one God in three Persons, we praise you and give you thanks for all the favors you have bestowed on us. Your goodness has preserved us until now. We offer you our whole being and in particular all our thoughts, words, and deeds, together with all the trials we may undergo this day. Give them your blessing. May your divine love animate them and may they serve your greater glory.

We make this morning offering in union with the divine intentions of Jesus Christ who offers himself daily in the holy sacrifice of the Mass, and in union with Mary, his Virgin Mother and our Mother, who was always the faithful handmaid of the Lord.

Amen.

Memorare

Remember, O most gracious Virgin Mary, that never was it known that anyone who fled to your protection, implored your help, or sought your protection was left unaided. Inspired with this confidence, we fly to you, O virgins of virgins, our Mother. To you we come, before you we stand, sinful and sorrowful. O Mother of the Word Incarnate, despise not our petitions, but in your mercy, hear and answer us. Amen.

Act of Faith

O my God, I firmly believe that you are one God in the three divine Persons, Father, Son, and Holy Spirit; I believe that your divine Son became man and died for our sins, and that he will come to judge the living and the dead. I believe these and all the truths which the holy Catholic Church teaches, because you revealed them. Who can neither deceive nor be deceived.

Act of Hope

O my God, relying on your infinite goodness and promises, I hope to obtain pardon of all my sins, and with the help of your grace, receive everlasting life, through the merits of Jesus Christ, my Lord and Redeemer.

Act of Love

O my God, I love you above all things, with my whole heart and soul, because you are all good and worthy of all my love. I love my neighbor as myself for the love of you. I forgive all who have injured me and I ask pardon of all whom I have injured.

Prayer to Our Redeemer

Soul of Christ, sanctify me;
Body of Christ, save me.
Blood of Christ, inebriate me;
Water from the side of Christ, wash me.
Passion of Christ, strengthen me.
O good Jesus hear me. Never permit me to be separated from you.
From the evil one protect me, at the hour of death call me, and bid me come to you that with your saints, I may praise you forever.
Amen.

Prayer to Jesus Crucified

Behold, my beloved and good Jesus. I cast myself upon my knees in your sight, and with the most fervent desire of my soul, I pray and beseech you, to impress upon my heart lively sentiments of faith, hope, and charity, with true repentance for my sins, and a firm desire of amendment; while with deep affection and grief of soul I consider within myself and mentally contemplate your most precious wounds, having before my eyes that which David, the prophet long ago spoke about you, my Jesus, "They have pierced my hands and my feet; I can count all my bones."

Act of Contrition

My God,
I am sorry for my sins with all my heart.
In choosing to do wrong
and failing to do good,
I have sinned against you
whom I should love above all things.
I firmly intend, with your help,
to do penance,
to sin no more,

and to avoid whatever leads me to sin.
Our savior Jesus Christ
suffered and died for us.
In his name, my God, have mercy. Amen.

Prayers for Interfaith Gatherings

The following prayers of invocation and blessings can be used to begin and conclude a prayer service of Christians from all denominations and those of other religious traditions. Other elements that may be included in such a service are: biblical readings and psalms, prayers of intercession, and the Lord's Prayer.

Prayers of Invocation

Leader: Blessed are you, Lord, God of all creation, whose goodness fills our hearts with joy. Blessed are you who have brought us together this day to work in harmony and peace. Strengthen us with your grace for you are Lord for ever and ever.
R: Amen.

Or:

Leader: In you, Lord our God, all things have
their beginning and end. Grace us with your
saving presence and aid us with your constant
help, now and for ever.

R: Amen.

Or:

Leader: Lord, may everything we do begin
with your inspiration and continue with your
help so that all our prayers and works may
begin and end in you. Glory and praise to you
for ever and ever.

R: Amen.

Blessings

Leader: May the God of every grace and blessing grant you joy and peace. May you rejoice
in God's protection, now and for ever.

R: Amen.

Or:

Leader: May God strengthen you and bring
your work to completion. May hope accompany your journey through the days to come.
May God's abiding presence be with you all

the days of your life.
R: Amen.
Or:

Leader: May the Lord bless you and keep you.
May his face shine upon you and be gracious
to you.
May he look upon you with kindness
and give you his peace.
R: Amen.

Prayers Near or At the Time of Death

The following prayers are from the Pastoral Care
of the Sick: Rite of Anointing and Viaticum. *They
may be led by the pastoral caregiver for and with
the dying person and his or her family at or near
the time of death.*

Commendation of the Dying

Go forth, Christian soul, from this world
in the name of God the almighty Father,
who created you,
in the name of Jesus Christ, Son of the living

God,
who suffered for you,
in the name of the Holy Spirit,
who was poured out upon you,
go forth, faithful Christian.

May you live in peace this day,
may your home be with God in Zion,
with Mary, the virgin Mother of God,
with Joseph, and all the angels and saints.

Or:

I commend you, my dear brother/sister,
    to almighty God,
and entrust you to your Creator.
May you return to him
who formed you from the dust of the earth.
May holy Mary, the angels, and all the saints
come to meet you as you go forth from this
life.
May Christ who was crucified for you
bring you freedom and peace.
May Christ who died for you
admit you into his garden of paradise.
May Christ, the true Shepherd,
acknowledge you as one of his flock.

May he forgive all your sins,
and set you among those he has chosen.
May you see your Redeemer face to face,
and enjoy the vision of God for ever. Amen.

Or:

Lord Jesus Christ, Savior of the world,
we pray for your servant N.,
and commend him/her to your mercy.
For his/her sake you came down from heaven;
receive him/her now into the joy of your
kingdom.

For though he/she has sinned,
he/she has not denied the Father, the Son, and
the Holy Spirit,
but has believed in God
and has worshipped his/her Creator. Amen.

Or:

Hail, holy Queen, Mother of mercy,
hail, our life, our sweetness, and our hope.
To you we cry, the children of Eve,
to you we send up our sighs,
mourning and weeping in this land of exile.
Turn, then, most gracious advocate,
your eyes of mercy toward us;

lead us home at last
and show us the blessed fruit of your womb,
Jesus:
O clement, O loving, O sweet Virgin Mary.

Prayer After Death

Saints of God, come to his/her aid!
Come to meet him/her, angels of the Lord!
R: Receive his/her soul and present him/her to
God the Most High.
May Christ, who called you, take you to himself;
may angels lead you to Abraham's side.
R: Receive his/her soul and present him/her to
God the Most High.
Give him/her eternal rest, O Lord,
and may your light shine on him/her for ever.
R: Receive his/her soul and present him/her to
God the Most High.

Let us pray.
All-powerful and merciful God,
we commend to you N., your servant.
In your mercy and love,
blot out the sins he/she has committed

through human weakness.
In this world he/she has died:
let him/her live with you for ever.
We ask this through Christ our Lord.
R: Amen.
Or:

God of mercy,
hear our prayers and be merciful to your
son/daughter N.,
whom you have called from this life.
Welcome him/her into the company of your
saints,
in the kingdom of light and peace.

We ask this through Christ our Lord. Amen.
Or:

Almighty and eternal God,
hear our prayers for your son/daughter N.,
whom you have called from this life to yourself.

Grant him/her light, happiness, and peace.
Let him/her pass in safety through the gates of
death,
and live for ever with all your saints in the
light you promised to Abraham
and to all his descendants in faith.

Guard him/her from all harm
and on that great day of resurrection and
reward
raise him/her up with all your saints.
Pardon his/her sins
and give him/her eternal life in your kingdom.

We ask this through Christ our Lord. Amen.

Or:

Loving and merciful God,
we entrust our brother/sister to your mercy.

You loved him/her greatly in this life:
now that he/she is freed from all its cares,
give him/her happiness and peace for ever.

The old order has passed away:
welcome him/her now into paradise
where there will be no more sorrow,
no more weeping or pain,
but only peace and joy
with Jesus, your Son,
and the Holy Spirit
for ever and ever. Amen.

Or:

God of our destiny,
into your hands we commend our
brother/sister.
We are confident that with all who have died
in Christ
he/she will be raised to life on the last day
and live with Christ for ever.

[We thank you for all the blessings
you gave him/her in this life
to show your fatherly care for all of us
and the fellowship which is ours with the
saints in Jesus Christ.]

Lord, hear our prayer:
welcome our brother/sister to paradise
and help us to comfort each other
with the assurance of our faith
until we all meet in Christ
to be with you and with our brother/sister
for ever.

We ask this through Christ our Lord. Amen.

Prayers for Family and Friends

God of all consolation,
in your unending love and mercy for us
you turn the darkness of death
into the dawn of new life.
Show compassion to your people in their
sorrow.

[Be our refuge and our strength
to lift us from the darkness of this grief
to the peace and light of your presence.]

Your Son, our Lord Jesus Christ,
by dying for us, conquered death
and by rising again, restored life.

May we then go forward eagerly to meet him,
and after our life on earth
be reunited with our brothers and sisters
where every tear will be wiped away.

We ask this through Christ our Lord. Amen.
Or:
Lord Jesus, our Redeemer,
you willingly gave yourself up to death

so that all people might be saved
and pass from death into a new life.
Listen to our prayers,
look with love on your people
who mourn and pray for their brother/sister
N.

Lord Jesus, holy and compassionate:
forgive N. his/her sins.
By dying you opened the gates of life
for those who believe in you:
do not let our brother/sister be parted from
you,
but by your glorious power
give him/her light, joy, and peace in heaven
where you live for ever and ever. Amen.

Human Services Directory

This section provides toll free numbers for agencies
which may be able to directly help older adults or you in your
pastoral care ministry. Several of the agencies have twenty-
four-hour service, most of the others have voice mail capabil-
ities so that you will be able to leave a message. Local agencies—like the area agency on aging, county departments of
health, Social Security offices, and hospitals—are not on the
list. These phone numbers can be accessed from your local
directory.

Air Ambulance Network 1-800-327-1966
Alcoholism Hotline 1-800-252-6465
Alzheimer's Disease 1-800-621-0379
AMC Cancer Research Center—
Cancer Info and Counseling 1-800-525-3777
American Academy of Allergy
and Immunology 1-800-822-2762
American Association of
Retired Persons (Legal Hotline)   . . .1-800-262-LAWS
American Cancer Society's
Cancer Response System 1-800-ACS-2345
American Council of the Blind 1-800-424-8666
American Diabetes Association 1-800-223-1138

American Foundation
for the Blind 1-800-232-5463
American Institute for
Preventive Medicine 1-800-345-2476
American Kidney Fund 1-800-622-9010
American Liver Foundation 1-800-223-0179
American Lung Foundation 1-800-352-0917
American Paralysis Association and
Spinal Cord 1-800-526-3456
American Society of Plastic and
Reconstructive Surgery 1-800-635-0635
American Trauma Society 1-800-556-7890
Army Benefits 1-800-336-4909
Arthritis Foundation 1-800-283-7800
Banking Complaints 1-800-722-2657
Better Hearing Institute 1-800-327-9355
Blind and Physically Handicapped
Information 1-800-424-9100
Books on Tape, Inc. 1-800-252-6996
Bureau of Consumer Protection 1-800-441-2555
Bureau of Professional and Occupational
Affairs—Dept. of State 1-800-822-2113
Bureau of Workers Compensation .. 1-800-482-2383
Center Careline 1-800-622-8922
Cancer Hotline
(American Cancer Society) 1-800-227-2345

Cancer Hotline, State 1-800-4-CANCER
Cancer Information Service 1-800-4-CANCER
Cardiac-Care Testing 1-800-822-4826
CEMP Counseling Services 1-800-652-0562
Center for Substance Abuse
Treatment Hotline 1-800-662-4357
Client Security Fund 1-800-962-4618
CONNECT Information Service . . . 1-800-692-7288
Crime Stoppers 1-800-472-8477
Deafness Research Foundation 1-800-535-3323
Delinquent Taxpayer Information . . 1-800-932-4621
Drug Abuse Information 1-800-662-4357
Drug and Alcohol Abuse Hotline . . . 1-800-932-0912
Eldercare Locator 1-800-677-1116
Employment Security 1-800-482-2383
EPA's Safe Drinking Water Hotline . .1-800-426-4791
Epilepsy Foundation of America . . . 1-800-332-1000
Fair Housing and Equal
Opportunity Office 1-800-669-9777
Federal Crime Insurance Program . . 1-800-638-8783
Federal Tax Information (IRS) . . . 1-800-829-FORM
Flood Insurance Program 1-800-638-6620
Food Stamps, cash assistance,
medical assistance 1-800-692-7462
Fraud Hotline 1-800-447-8477
Fraud Task Force 1-800-424-5454

Hearing Aid Helpline/National
Hearing Aid Society 1-800-521-5247
Hearing Helpline 1-800-327-9355
Health Information Center 1-800-336-4797
Higher Education and Adult Training for People
with Handicaps Resource Center . . . 1-800-544-3284
Hospice Link Service 1-800-331-1620
Hotline Information 1-800-555-1212
Housing Discrimination 1-800-669-9777
HUD USER 1-800-483-2209
Income Maintenance Hotline 1-800-692-7462
Information or Complaints of Fraud of
Medigap Insurance 1-800-638-6833
Insurance Consumer Information . . 1-800-222-1750
Insurance Information Institute 1-800-942-4242
Internal Revenue Service 1-800-829-1040
Job Accommodation Network 1-800-526-7234
Lawyer Referral 1-800-4-LAWYER
Legal Hotline for
Older Americans 1-800-262-5297
License Tags for the Handicapped . . 1-800-932-4600
Lifeline Systems 1-800-451-0525
Living Bank International (organ and tissue
donor bank) 1-800-528-2971
Major Appliance Consumer
Action Panel 1-800-621-0477

MECA 1-800-950-6322
Medic Alert 1-800-344-3226
Medic Alert Foundation
International 1-800-ID-ALERT
Medical Insurance Fraud 1-800-438-2478
Medicare 1-800-382-1274
Medicare Complaints 1-800-368-5779
Missing Children 1-800-235-3535
Missing Children Help Center 1-800-872-5437
Mortgage Assistance and
Foreclosure Hotline 1-800-342-2397
Myasthenia Gravis Foundation 1-800-541-5454
National AIDS Clearinghouse 1-800-458-5231
National Alcohol Hotline 1-800-ALCOHOL
National Alliance for the
Mentally Ill 1-800-950-NAMI
National Association for
Hearing and Speech 1-800-638-8255
National Association for
Hispanic Elderly 1-800-953-8553
National Association for
Sickle Cell Disease, Inc. 1-800-421-8453
National Association of Area
Agencies on Aging 1-800-667-1116
National Asthma Center 1-800-222-5864
National Bone Marrow Registry . .1-800-MARROW2

National Center for Missing
and Exploited Children 1-800-843-5678
. . . . .1-800-826-7653 (TDD)
National Center for Stuttering 1-800-221-2483
National Cocaine Hotline 1-800-COCAINE
National Council on Aging, Inc. . . . 1-800-424-9046
National Council on Alcoholism
and Drug Dependence, Inc. 1-800-NCA-CALL
National Eye Care Project 1-800-222-3937
National Foundation for
Depressive Illness 1-800-248-4344
National Fraud Information 1-800-876-7060
National Head Injury Foundation . . 1-800-444-6443
National Headache Foundation 1-800-843-2256
National Health
Information Center 1-800-336-4797
National Highway Traffic Safety Administration
and Safety Auto Line 1-800-424-9393
National Hospice Organization 1-800-658-8898
National Insurance
Consumer Helpline 1-800-942-4242
National Kidney Foundation 1-800-622-9010
National Library for Blind
and Handicapped 1-800-424-9100
National Literacy Hotline 1-800-228-8813
National Marfan Foundation 1-800-862-7326

National Organizations of
Social Security Claimants Reps 1-800-431-2804
National Parkinson Foundation, Inc. . . 1-800-327-4545
National Response Center 1-800-424-8802
National Safety Council 1-800-621-7619
National Spinal Cord
Injury Association 1-800-962-9629
Organ Donations Hotline 1-800-528-2971
Organ Donor Hotline 1-800-24-DONOR
Pesticide Hotlines 1-800-858-7378
Center for Organ Recovery and
Core Education 1-800-366-6777
Product Safety Hotline 1-800-638-2772
Program/Books for the
Blind/Handicapped 1-800-424-9100
Recorded Books 1-800-638-1304
Recording for the Blind 1-800-221-4792
Social Security Disability 1-800-772-1213
Spinal Bifida Association
  of America 1-800-621-3141
Telephone Systems 1-800-682-6857
The Alliance for Aging Research . . . 1-800-639-2421
The Gray Panthers Project Fund . . . 1-800-280-5362
U.S. Department of Defense 1-800-424-9098
U.S. Committee for UNICEF 1-800-345-6650

U.S. Department of Housing and
Urban Development 1-800-669-9777
U.S. Food Safety Hotline 1-800-535-4555
U.S. General Accounting Office
Fraud Hotline 1-800-424-5454
U.S. Officer of Special Counsel 1-800-872-9855
U.S. Social Security Administration 1-800-772-1213
Veteran's Outreach 1-800-352-0915
Water Test Corps. 1-800-426-8378
Welfare Office of Income
Maintenance 1-800-692-7462
Whistle Blowers Hotline
(GAO Fraud Hotline) 1-800-424-5454
Women's Community
Health Center 1-800-327-9880
Women's Sports Hotline 1-800-227-3988
Workman's Compensation 1-800-482-2383
Y-Me National Organization for Breast Cancer
Information and Support 1-800-221-2141

Home-Health Hotline Numbers

The federal government has established the following state-operated phone numbers to collect information on home health agencies in each state that are certified by Medicare. You can call the appropriate number to report complaints about patient care at agencies in your area.

	State	Hotline Number
REGION I		
	Connecticut	1-800-828-9769
	Maine	1-800-621-8222
	Massachusetts	1-800-462-5540
	New Hampshire	1-800-621-6232
	Rhode Island	1-800-277-2788
	Vermont	1-800-564-1612
REGION II		
	New Jersey	1-800-792-9770
	New York	1-800-628-5972

REGION III

Delaware	1-800-942-7373
District of Columbia	202-727-7873
Maryland	1-800-492-6005
Pennsylvania	1-800-277-2788
Virginia	1-800-955-1819
West Virginia	1-800-442-2888

REGION IV

Alabama	1-800-225-9770
Florida	1-800-962-6014
Georgia	1-800-326-0291
Kentucky	1-800-635-6290
Mississippi	1-800-227-7308
North Carolina	1-800-624-3004
Puerto Rico	809-721-5710
South Carolina	1-800-922-6735
Tennessee	1-800-541-7367
Virgin Islands	809-774-2991

REGION V

Illinois	1-800-252-4343
Indiana	1-800-227-6334
Michigan	1-800-882-6006
Minnesota	1-800-369-7994
Ohio	1-800-342-0553
Wisconsin	1-800-642-6552

REGION VI

Arkansas	1-800-223-0340
Louisiana	1-800-327-3419
New Mexico	1-800-752-8649
Oklahoma	1-800-234-7258
Texas	1-800-228-1570

REGION VII

Iowa	1-800-281-4920
Kansas	1-800-842-0078
Missouri	1-800-877-6485
Nebraska	1-800-245-5832

REGION VIII

Colorado	1-800-842-8826
Montana	1-800-762-4618
North Dakota	1-800-545-8256
South Dakota	1-800-592-1861
Utah	1-800-999-7339
Wyoming	1-800-548-7367

REGION IX

| Arizona | 1-800-221-9968 |
| California | |

Northern Region:
  Sacramento District Office
                1-800-554-0354

Chico District Office
1-800-554-0350
Santa Rosa District Office
1-800-554-0349
Berkeley District Office
1-800-554-0352
Daly City District Office
1-800-554-0353

Southern Region:
Los Angeles District Office
1-800-228-1019
San Jose District Office
1-800-554-0351
Fresno District Office
1-800-554-0351
Ventura District Office
1-800-547-8267
Orange County District Office
1-800-228-5234
San Diego District Office
1-800-824-0613
San Bernardino District Office
1-800-344-2896

Hawaii	1-800-762-5949
Nevada	1-800-225-3414

REGION X

Alaska	907-563-0037
Idaho	1-800-345-1453
Oregon	1-800-542-5186
Washington	1-800-633-6828

Bibliography

Bauer, Cecile. *Caregiver's Gethsemane: When A Loved One Longs to Die*. New York: Paulist Press, 1995.

Callanan, Maggie and Patricia Kelly. *Final Gifts*. New York, NY: Bantam Books, 1993.

Champlin, Joseph M. and Susan Champlin Tayter. *A Thoughtful Word, A Healing Touch, A Guide for Visiting the Sick*. Mystic, CT: Twenty-Third Publications, 1995.

Condray, Sydney. *Assembled in Christ, 44 Liturgies with Lay Presiders*. Mystic, CT: Twenty-Third Publications, 1993.

DeGidio, OSM, Sandra. *Prayer Services for the Elderly: Giving Comfort and Joy*. Mystic, CT: Twenty-Third Publications, 1996.

Dubyoski, B.A., Maryann. *Strategies and Programs: Involving Elders in Your Parish Community*. Cleveland, OH: Office of Aging, Federation of Catholic Services of the Diocese of Cleveland, 1984.

Hover, Margot. *Caring for Yourself When Caring for Others*. Mystic, CT: Twenty-Third Publications, 1993.

LeFever, Marlene D. *Creative Teaching Methods*. Elgin, IL: David C. Cook Publishing, 1985.

Miller, Kent C. *Ministry to the Homebound . . . A Ten-Session Training Course*. San Jose, CA: Resource Publications, 1995.

National Conference of Catholic Bishops. *Pastoral Care of the Sick*. New York: Catholic Book Publishing Co., 1983.

Normile, Patti. *Prayers for Caregivers*. Cincinnati, OH: St. Anthony Messenger Press, 1995.

Nouwen, Henri J.M. *Can You Drink the Cup?* Notre Dame, IN: Ave Maria Press, 1996.

Older Adult Ministry: A Resource for Program Development. Atlanta, GA: Presbyterian Publishing House, 1987.

Peace Be with YOU. Ligouri, MO: Ligouri Publications, 1987.

Pilla, D.D., Anthony M. *A Pastoral Letter to Older Adults and Loved Ones*. Diocese of Cleveland, 1984.

Reilly, Maria. *Now That I Am Old: Meditations on the Meaning of Life*. Mystic, CT: Twenty-Third Publications, 1994.

Rockers, O.S.F., Dolores and Kenneth J. Pierre, Ph.D. *Shared Ministry: An Integrated Approach to Leadership and Service*. Winona, MN: St. Mary's Press, 1984.

Sanders, J. Oswald. *Enjoying Your Best Years: Staying Young While Growing Older*. Grand Rapids, MI: Discovery House Publishers, 1993.

Tan, Sang-Yang and John Ortberg, Jr. *Coping with Depression: The Common Cold of Emotional Life*. Grand Rapids, MI: Baker Books, 1995.

Final Reflections for Pastoral Caregivers

As we look ahead, we can imagine hundreds of people reaching out to help one another, sharing in each other's sorrows and joys, and actively spreading the message of God's love. This is an exciting vision.

Unfortunately, there is one major glitch. We have to realize that there will be times when we will be frustrated, or even feel hopeless. We may feel unappreciated, confused or feel that we are being used. These feelings are normal. They are neither good nor bad. Nor do they reflect the degree of our caring as a pastoral caregiver. What is important is how we handle these feelings.

At times like these, we need to open ourselves to God's presence dwelling within us. Ask God to do for us what we cannot do for ourselves.

Surrender ourselves to the Divine Power within us, and pray to the Holy Spirit to increase our understanding and to enlighten our minds.

This book has offered you many suggestions for ministering to older adults. These suggestions may be altered in accordance with the unique structure, resources, and needs of your community.

In order to hold onto our initial enthusiasm, we need to keep our vision before us. Remember that since the role of a pastoral caregiver is spiritual, we must ask for help from God and others. It is easy to get into a state of constant worry or anxiety, thinking we should be able to do everything ourselves. By asking for help, we will ensure our quality pastoral caregiving.

We can best help others when we rely on others. Be specific and positive. Ask others to help you with your tasks. Being a martyr benefits no one. We must take time for ourselves. We must take time each day to pray. Studies show that sacrificing oneself in the care of another and removing pleasurable events from one's life can lead to emotional exhaustion and burn out.

When done in the right spirit and with God's help, the benefits of this ministry of pastoral care for older adults will give us new satisfaction, an opportunity to make new friendships, and a confidence in our God-given abilities.

May the Lord bless you and keep you always.

Appendix

Dear Brothers and Sisters in Christ,

I have a favor to ask of you. After much prayer and consultation I feel the Holy Spirit is calling me to write another book. Before any new product is put on the market in the secular world, there is extensive research. Jesus asked his apostles what people thought of him before Jesus put his confidence in Peter. I need your assistance. Your cooperation is essential in helping me determine your spiritual needs.

This survey below is intended to provide the author with information on which to base research for a new publication on the spirituality of older adults. The first 500 people who fill out this survey will receive a copy of the new book free of charge. You may mail your answers to one or more of the questions below. Any input you can give to me will be greatly appreciated.

1. What is the church saying to you today?
2. What reinforced your convictions in the church since 1960?
3. How did you make your spiritual adjustments to the post-Vatican II church?
4. What in your faith sustains you now?
5. What events or happenings in your life helped you in your relationship with God and others?
6. How do you cope with others of different values?
7. What helps you from the past to understand spiritually how to experience and face the events of your "golden years"?
8. What could help us better to understand our death and dying process?
9. What helps a person spiritually who is living as a handicapped older adult?
10. What is the meaning of pain and suffering—for you?
11. How do you image God?
12. Where do you see God's activity in your life?

Feel free to share a story of your spiritual journey. This could be a story of a significant turning point in your life that helps you make the adjustments of growing old spiritually. Would you give me, Father J. Daniel Dymski, the author, permission to use and share your story in the new book? I will use your first name or a fictitious name if you allow me to put your spiritual experience in print.

This research may be accomplished in libraries. But the better way to learn is through knowing the faith experience of others.

Your Brother in Christ,
Father J. Daniel Dymski
Sacred Heart Church
816 West 26th Street
Erie, PA 16508
814-480-8994
Email: frdymski@aol.com
URL: www.frdan.com

About the Author:

Fr. J. Daniel Dymski is a priest in the diocese of Erie, Pennsylvania. Fr. Dymski has spent most of his thirty-eight years in the priesthood involved in some way in the pastoral care of older adults. Most recently Fr. Dymski was the coordinator of pastoral services to nursing homes for the Erie diocese.

Printed in the United States
104354LV00001B/37/A

9 780877 936732